# PROVENCE
# & CÔTE D'AZUR

Produced by AA Publishing

European Regional Guide

**AA**

**• CREDITS**

2

Written by Sarah Le Tellier,
Richard Sale, Hazel Evans

Copy editors: Janet Tabinski, Nia
Williams

Edited, designed and produced by
AA Publishing. Maps © The
Automobile Association 1993.

Distributed in the United Kingdom
by AA Publishing, Fanum House,
Basingstoke, Hampshire, RG21
2EA.

The contents of this publication
are believed correct at the time of
printing. Nevertheless, the
publishers cannot accept
responsibility for errors or
omissions, or for changes in details
given. We have tried to ensure
accuracy in this guide, but things
do change and we would be
grateful if readers would advise us
of any inaccuracies they may
encounter.

© The Automobile Association 1993.

A CIP catalogue record for this
book is available from the British
Library.

ISBN  0 7495 0582 6

Published by The Automobile
Association.

Colour separation: Daylight Colour
Art Pte, Singapore

Printed by Printers Trento S.R.L.,
Italy

Cover picture: **Lavender fields**
Opposite: **St-Tropez, Côte d'Azur**
Pages 4-5: **Gordes, Vaucluse**

# ·CONTENTS·

## FEATURES

## MAPS

*The main entries in this book are cross-referenced to the regional map on pages 112–13. All heights on maps are in metres.*

# ·INTRODUCTION·

This guide reveals the true character and flavour of Provence, its people, legends and traditions, with detailed information and special features, illustrated throughout in full colour.

Specially drawn, easy-to-follow maps accompany over 25 walks and tours which take you out and about into the countryside as well as round the most popular towns and cities.

With practical information and a glossary of useful words and phrases, this is an invaluable guide to visiting this fascinating region of France.

# ·HISTORY·

Provence is one of the largest regions in France, stretching as it does from beyond the delta of the Rhône to the Alps. It is a land of tremendous contrasts, encompassing more than 325km of coastline dotted with fashionable beaches, as well as fertile plains, valleys and desolate mountain ranges – and its vivid history is firmly written into the landscape. There are few other places in Europe where the effect of history is so evident, in the buildings, the dialects and even the way of life.

Charlemagne (below) brought a brief period of peace to Provence, giving the land to his son Lothaire

## BEGINNINGS

First the Celts and the Ligurians made Provence their home, then came the Greeks, known as the Phocaeans, who founded *Massalia* (Marseille) as a trading port and established a colony there. They are thought to have given the Rhône river its name, and established a number of other outposts, notably at Arles and Nice. It was the Greeks who planted the first vineyards and olive groves. But they were under constant attack from the wild tribes inland. And when the Celts put *Massalia* under pressure, the Greeks, with their empire on the verge of collapse, asked Rome for help. This was an opportunity that the Romans could not resist: they came to *Massalia*'s aid – and so began their conquest of the South of France.

## INVADERS

The greatest period in the region's history was undoubtedly during the time of the Romans. Ruling for almost 600 years, the conquerors brought with them a stability that was hitherto unknown, creating an infrastructure of towns and settlements and, most important of all, roads. They also built canals and aqueducts to distribute much-needed water to their cities.

Once the Romans were forced to abandon Gaul – due in the main to a collapse in their own internal economy back in Rome – Provence became once again a battleground for marauding tribes. The barbarian hordes, the Franks and the Visigoths, the Vikings, and the Moors – Arabs who came over from North Africa – devastated everything before them. Finally, in 536, the province was ceded to the Franks; 200 years later their most famous king, Charlemagne, was to rule it at first with great ferocity.

Then came the invasions of the Saracens from North Africa, and the whole province became a battlefield once again. Peace did not return until Charlemagne decided to divide his empire between his children and gave Provence to his eldest son, Lothaire. But it was a far from united kingdom, with battling warlords fighting over their particular pieces of territory. During this time Provence became a place the Knights Templar passed through on their way to the Crusades, and where troubadours roamed the land, singing their romantic poetry. Over the years to come, the province came under the rule of numerous counts, one of them the

Count of Barcelona, whose name was given to the small town in the Alpes-de-Haute-Provence that we now know as Barcelonette.

Then came the turn of Charles of Anjou, who invoked the protection of the Holy Roman Empire. And in 1305 French-born Pope Clement V decided to move his court to Avignon, a city from which the popes were to reign for most of the 14th century.

## PROSPERITY AND BLOODSHED

The Hundred Years' War left the province almost untouched, but the Counts of Savoy did succeed in taking some of the countryside along their border which, including the towns of Nice and Menton, was to remain under Italian rule until 1860.

One of the most loved rulers of Provence was the Good King René, who died in 1480. He created a flourishing economy, starting the silkworm industry, which gave employment to people in the remote hill villages. He established a court at Aix, elevating its status to rival that of Avignon. In the early 1500s a parliament was held there. It was from Aix that an order went out triggering off a long history of religious bloodshed. As news of the Reformation spread to the South, the Protestants became strongest in the Lubéron. Many were massacred as a result of their new beliefs; but the worst incident was when the newly formed Parliament of Provence at Aix ordered that the whole village of Merindol should be destroyed.

## PLAGUE AND REVOLUTION

The 18th century was a time of pestilence. More than 100,000 people died in Provence alone during the Great Plague, brought, it is said, by a ship that landed in Marseille in 1720. With this decimated population, farms were neglected and villages left deserted. The century ended turbulently with the French Revolution. Provence can claim credit for the French national anthem, *La Marseillaise*, for a group of volunteers, who marching from Marseille to Paris, took a battle hymn used by French troops against the Germans and made it their own.

In 1790 Provence was divided into three *départements* by the newly formed Revolutionary government: Bouches-du-Rhône in the south and west, Basse-Alpes in the North, and the Var. The following year, these were joined by Avignon and the Comtat Venaissin.

## THE EMPEROR

Then came the time of the Emperor. Napoleon always had affection for Provence, for it was to Nice that he came with his bride Josephine, only to leave her after two days to join battle in Italy. So it was not surprising that he returned to his old haunts in 1814, when attempting to stage a comeback after being forced into exile on the island of Elba. He returned to the Provençal coast at Golfe-Juan, calling himself the Emperor of the French (a commemorative stone marks the spot today). But his mission was doomed to failure. The Provençals did not welcome him, so he took his army from Cannes up over the Alpes-Maritimes, making for Paris, only to be defeated at Waterloo later in the year. The road that he used – the N85, which goes through Sisteron and Dignes – is known to this day as the Route Napoléon.

## TRANSFORMATION

The late 1800s and the turn of the century saw the transformation of the Provençal coast into a holiday area as transportation improved, especially with the arrival of rail travel in 1864. In the 20th century, two world wars have inevitably left their mark. In the 1940s, locals put up a brave resistance during two years of German occupation, and many martyrs were made, notably Jean Moulin, who has a route named after him. Many innocent people suffered at that time. Stark evidence can be seen, for instance, in one small village in the Lubéron, St-Saturnin-d'Apt. Here the main square is dominated by a memorial on a wall packed with bullet holes made when hostages were shot. Liberated by the Americans in 1944, Provence has once again, in the second half of the century, taken its place as one of the most popular tourist venues in France.

The imperial divorce (1809): Napoleon left Josephine in Provence while he joined his army in Italy

# GEOGRAPHY AND CLIMATE

As the countryside south of Lyon changes from the cold grey colours of the north, Provence begins. Traditional red-tile roofs brighten the houses, and the landscape becomes a patchwork of vineyards, olive orchards and fields of lavender and sunflowers. Villages and towns are shaded by plane trees, the sun shines with a special brilliance. And sunshine is what you get for most of the year in this part of France, albeit with low temperatures at times.

Canoeists take advantage of the dramatic Gorges du Verdon scenery

## HILLS AND MOUNTAINS

Provence is dominated by several mountain ranges which dictate its climate. To the north, cutting Provence off from the rest of France, there is the Ventoux chain, presided over by Mont Ventoux, and, around Digne and Sisteron, the Alpes-de-Haute-Provence. The countryside here is craggy, mountainous and wild, with deep gorges edged with twisting, hairpin roads. The hills are clothed by the *garrigue*, (Mediterranean scrubland), and above the snow line there are stunted forests of pine.

Further south, separated by the Vaucluse plateau, are the Petit and the Grand Lubéron ranges edged by the Durance river and, nearer the Rhône, the Alpilles, needle-like limestone outcrops. Near Aix, Cézanne's mountain, Mte Ste-Victoire, towers over the neighbouring country-side, ending in an accordion-shaped ridge, stretching eastwards. The flat coastal strip – which varies from sharp cliffs, the *calanques* between Marseille and Cassis and beaches of sand or shingle – is backed first by the Massif des Maures, which stands guard over St-Tropez, then the craggy Estérel Mountains, and finally the Alpes-Maritimes, snow-covered in winter, protecting the Riviera.

## THE VALLEYS

In between these mountain ranges there are wide, fertile valleys like those of the Vaucluse, growing vines and early fruit and vegetable crops. In spring the cherry trees make a white carpet of flowers, with an underlay of colourful wild flowers in spring. And in autumn the valleys turn red-bronze with the dying leaves on the vines.

Around the Rhône valley, the landscape tends to be flat and unremarkable, with vineyards, olive groves and fields of melons sheltered by windbreaks of bamboo. The Camargue, in southwest Provence, has a look and a climate quite different from the rest of the *département*. The terrain is totally flat, with swampy ground punctuated by lagoons where water and sky seem to merge into one, and the sea backed by sand dunes. Here you'll find France's lowest rainfall, which contrasts with the humidity of the climate.

The Rhône, one of France's greatest waterways, is the main river in Provence, but of equal importance to the people who live there is its tributary, the Durance, which snakes across the province from south of Avignon and skirts the south side of the Lubéron mountains near Cadenet and Pertuis before swinging north near the Gorges du Verdon. Almost bereft of water in summer, the Durance can become a raging torrent after heavy rain.

## CLIMATE

Geographically speaking, Provence is the most northerly edge of the Sahara Desert, now cut off from North Africa by the Mediterranean. And this is reflected in its climate. In summer the heat of the Sahara makes its way north, giving a long, hot, rainless season. But in the relatively short winter the weather can get fiercely cold: the warm desert air retreats in the path of cold blasts from northern Europe. Up in the mountains, violent thunderstorms in spring and autumn will often cut off electricity and phones; in winter the vineyards can be clothed in snow.

There is no gentle change from one season to the next; things alter abruptly. In springtime, one evening you'll be shivering in the chill winds of winter, and the next the warm daytime temperature lingers on, and you know that summer is on the way.

Temperatures vary by several degrees between the coastal strip and inland areas. In January and February, while the temperature will seldom be above 11°C up in the hills, on the Côte d'Azur it is more likely to be 13°C. As spring and summer come, you can expect temperatures about 2°C higher in places like the Lubéron than down on the coast. Higher up in the mountains there is always a breeze even on the hottest days in summer, but in winter conditions are harsh.

Provence is famous for its winds – there are said to be almost 30 different kinds. The most famous of them all is the Mistral, which funnels from the north down the Rhône, leaving shutters banging and people irritable. It comes mainly in spring and autumn, usually lasts two or three days, and brings with it clear blue skies. By the time it reaches the east, the Mistral has lost most of its strength and, finally, the towering Alpes-Maritimes deflect it from the Riviera lying below.

The second strong wind is the Sirocco, a warm wind from North Africa that carries with it desert sand, depositing it on the Provençal countryside. Less forceful than the Mistral, it can seem suffocating in summer. Two other winds bring rain: the showery Marin from the southeast, and the Labech from the west, which brings heavy storms.

## WHEN TO GO

Wherever you are going, spring is delightful when the wild flowers come out and the cherry trees are in blossom, but the temperature may not be high enough for sunbathing. April and May bring blue skies, but also the Mistral. June and September are the best months to visit. Then it is warm, but without that dry, suffocating heat that demands a daily siesta. October is a tricky month; it may give you a perfect Indian summer or you may get four or five days of rain at a stretch. In winter the sun still shines, but nights can be freezing cold. Daytime, however, can be delightful, and it is not unknown for people to eat their lunch outside on Christmas Day.

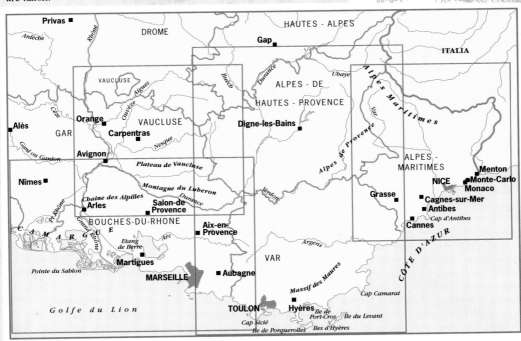

# PEOPLE AND TRADITIONS

Despite the common perception that people of the south have a *mañana* mentality, the average Provençal works hard. But he plays hard too, for the people know how to enjoy themselves – whether it is a game of *boules*, or a drink under the plane trees in the village square, or one of the many *bals musettes* (dances) and festivals that are held throughout the summer.

## TRADITION AND SUPERSTITION

Almost every village has a celebration of some sort, usually a dance held out in the open air, and it is well worth looking out for the posters advertising them. The Provençals are a superstitious race, and even today many people in the outlying villages believe in the evil eye. Many a doorway has the hand of Fatima over it to ward off evil spirits, a custom that dates back to the days when the Moors invaded the south. And two villages in the Vaucluse – Méthamis, near Mormoiron in the Mont Ventoux area, and Lacoste in the Lubéron – are still believed today to house witches and sorcerers in their midst. Vauvenargues, the village near Mte Ste-Victoire where Picasso lived, is also thought to be a place where witchcraft is still practised.

In ancient times the villagers of Provence had their own way of dealing with the occult: the *démascaire*, their own version of a witch doctor, who was not only able to exorcise evil spells but practised simple medicine too. The *démascaires* were often shepherds who, because of their lonely life and frequent absence from the village, were credited with supernatural powers.

Menton celebrates its *Fête du Citron* in February with displays of lemons, oranges and flowers

## FEASTS AND FESTIVALS

The average Provençal welcomes any excuse to dress up and celebrate, so festivals have always played an important part in local life. They start at Easter with a festival at Arles. Then, every month in the summer there is something on, from the Ochre Festival at Roussillon around Pentecost, right through to the Rice Festival in Arles in September, celebrating the harvest from the nearby Camargue. A number of them, not unnaturally, are concerned with wine. There is the Feast of St Mark, the patron saint of wine growers, for instance, at Villeneuve-lès-Avignon at the end of April. And the wine is blessed in a procession at Boulbon on 1 June. At the beginning of the same month, a wine festival held at Courthézon includes a sermon preached in the Provençal language: Provençal is also spoken at the Winegrowers Festival at Séguret at the end of August. Nîmes has its wine harvest festival on the last weekend in September.

## SPANISH INFLUENCE

In the Rhône valley, and to the west of the Rhône, the Spanish influence makes itself felt with *ferias* and *corridas* (bullfights), which are held in the summer. In Nîmes they start in June. And, after a *feria* at Easter, Arles starts the summer season with a special

*course à la cocarde d'or* (golden rosette race) on the first Monday in July. Tarascon also stages bullfights in the last week of June. At most places the bull survives the spectacle, but in Arles the beasts are not so lucky.

## THE CAMARGUE

The Camargue has its own distinctive festivals, starting with one for the *gardians* (cowboys) in late April. The gypsies from the area all gather at Stes-Maries-de-la-Mer on the Mediterranean coast for their annual pilgrimage on 24 and 25 May. If you are lucky you will see some of the traditional dances, enacted to the music of a pipe and a *tambourin*, a type of side drum. Stes-Maries-de-la-Mer comes into the limelight again at the end of October, when the sea is blessed at a special ceremony, and the gypsies celebrate once again. This is a little-known ceremony that takes place on the Sunday nearest to 22 October, a good time to see the local colour when there are fewer tourists around.

## TRADITIONAL DRESS

It is at the festivals that you will see people in traditional Provençal dress. Costumes are on view in a number of museums, particularly the Muséon Arlaten in Arles. In the past, the women of Arles were not only considered to be the most beautiful, but also the best dressed. And their colourful costume typifies traditional Provençal clothes: a bell-shaped skirt, often with a frill at the bottom made in the bright Provençal prints, and, underneath, numerous petticoats in complex quilting patterns echoing those on the *boutis*, the quilts on their beds.

With the skirt goes a long-sleeved blouse and a *fichu*, or shawl-like collar edged with lace. The wearer's hair is fixed in a *chignon* on the top of her head crowned by one of a variety of caps, some edged with lace or ribbons. The men wear thick linen or canvas trousers, a red or black cummerbund and a white shirt with a knotted tie.

## RELIGIOUS FESTIVALS

The Provençal people are very devout, and nowhere can this be seen more than in the churches, where at Christmas time there are beautifully decorated cribs with little carved figures. The idea of the traditional Provençal *santons*, – small figures illustrating the Nativity – came from Jean Louis Lagnel of Marseille, at the time of the French Revolution. A carver of statues for churches and gravestones, Lagnel thought of making small figures that ordinary people could buy and display in their homes. Now the *santons* have become a popular tourist buy.

Villages vie with one another to produce more and more elaborate church scenes. In some places, notably l'Isle-sur-la-Sorgue, Marseille, and some mountain villages, live actors present a mimed Nativity scene for the congregation at the Christmas Midnight Mass. At Les Baux, in the church of St Vincent, they go one stage further and bring a baby lamb into the church together with caped shepherds. It is at services such as this that the hymns and prayers are often conducted in the Provençal language. In midsummer at the Chapel of Ste-Radegonde, in the Lubéron valley, much of the service in honour of the sainted nun of that name is held in Provençal.

## PROVENÇAL REVIVAL

The sense of regional identity is strong. There are signs of a revival of the Provençal language, in which *le* is replaced by *lou*, and many words have a Roman look about them. Road signs are appearing everywhere in traditional Provençal as well as classic French. It was the poet Mistral who painstakingly collected all he could find about the old Provençal (or Occitain) language and issued a dictionary, first published in 1878, which is still used as a reference book today. Old Provençal is now included in some schools' curricula, and an Institute of Occitanian Studies has been set up to study the language. Meanwhile, the influence of the original tongue can also be encountered in the villages where French is spoken with a thick Provençal dialect and a different emphasis on words.

While welcoming foreigners on the whole, the people of Provence have a deep distrust of Parisians. They have never forgiven them for imposing the French language on the South in 1539 with the Edict of Villers-Cotterets.

Many Provençals today are under the illusion that once Europe is truly united, everyone will have to speak English, so English conversation classes are all full. You will find, more and more, that in Provençal shops and restaurants the locals make an effort to practise their *anglais*.

People of Provence at work in Marseille's old harbour

# •VAUCLUSE•

**For those travelling south through France on the A7 (the Autoroute du Soleil) or on the N7 – each of which hugs the Rhône river south of Lyon – Mont Ventoux acts as a frontier post for Provence. Ventoux stands in Vaucluse, the northernmost of the *départements* that make up what might be termed the real Provence: the land of Aix and Marseille, Arles and the Camargue, and the Avignon of the popes.**

Avignon lies in Vaucluse, as do Carpentras, once home to a thriving Jewish community, and the fine Roman city of Orange. The contrast in the histories of these three cities is also found in the landscapes of the *département*, which are no less interesting than those which lie to the south and offer a little more variety.

The name Vaucluse is derived from *Vallis Clausa* ('the closed valley'), a name applied from Roman times to the valley of the River Sorgue. This river is created by water draining into the high limestone plateau at the centre of the *département*, water which mixes underground and then emerges from a pool beneath high cliffs above Fontaine-de-Vaucluse. The water's resurgence offers one of the *département*'s most spectacular sights in spring, when heavy rain turns it into a raging torrent.

In time the name of the valley was applied to the plateau itself, and then to the entire region. The plateau, which falls away from Mont Ventoux to the north to reach the Coulon valley, is itself a land of contrasts. Its

limestone is honeycombed with caves, some of which have been followed almost 500m underground. The land at the plateau's edge is very fertile, especially at the southwestern corner where there is some of the finest vegetable- and fruit-growing land in France, with Cavaillon being home to the country's

largest market for the produce.

Further east, near Roussillon, there are huge beds of ochre which have been quarried, resulting in a unique and dramatic landscape. Set between the two is Gordes, one of the region's most photogenic villages, while in the Coulon valley itself, Apt can lay claim to one of the best craft markets in Provence.

The northern section of the plateau, together with land to the north of Mont Ventoux, formed the Comtat Venaissin, land ceded to the papacy by France in the early Middle Ages in exchange for support during the religious conflict known as the Albigensian Crusade. The existence of a part of the Papacy in France was to prove useful to one French pope when he decided that the bloody squabbles in central Italy were not to his liking. It is to this pope, Clement V, and several of his successors that we owe the grandest and one of the most interesting buildings in Vaucluse – the Palace of the Popes in Avignon. To the Avignon Papacy we also owe one of the oddest aspects of Vaucluse. North of Mont Ventoux the Papacy acquired land near Valréas. This land lay outside the Comtat Venaissin, and the Papacy started to buy further land in an effort to link it with its southern holdings. The French king vetoed further purchases, however, leaving the Valréas Enclave – a land of lavender and herb fields – as an island inside France. Today the Enclave is a Vauclusian island sitting within the *département* of Drôme.

Mont Ventoux, the Provence signpost, is one of France's most famous peaks, a mountain of

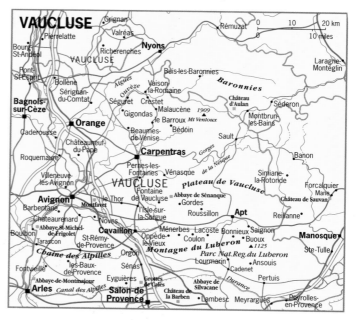

changing scenery, from low-lying woodland to summit bareness. On its southern flank there are a number of delightful villages and the fine river scenery of the Gorge de la Nesque. To the west lie the jagged peaks of the Dentelles de Montmirail, on the slopes of which grow the vines for one of France's newest AOC wines.

The more famous wine-growing area lies to the east, where the vineyards of Châteauneuf-du-Pape overlook the Rhône. At the time of the Avignon popes the Rhône was the border between France and the Holy Roman Empire, and it still forms an impressive frontier between Vaucluse and Gard. It is an impressive river, soft and picturesque on clear days in summer, but less friendly when driven by the Mistral or filled with the meltwaters of winter's snow.

The Rhône valley has always been one of the great highways of Europe, so it is no surprise to discover that one of the Romans' major roads followed it to reach Lyon and central France. The Romans established a town at Orange, building a theatre there that has survived simply because its back wall was so sturdy that it was incorporated in later defensive works. No matter – for the historically minded visitor, the Orange theatre is now one of the highlights of Provence. The same visitor might also go a few miles northeast to Vaison-la-Romaine to see the excavated remains of one of France's most complete Roman towns. Sadly, in September 1992 the village and some of the remains were badly damaged when the Ouvèze, swollen with rain from a severe storm, broke its banks, killing over 30 people.

Other such villages can be found all over the Lubéron Hills, whose southern slopes go down to the Durance, the river that divides Vaucluse from Bouches-du-Rhône. The Lubéron is one of the least visited areas in Provence, but deserves to be more popular. In medieval times the village folk of the area, being mainly Protestant, suffered badly, enduring long sieges, massacres and mass transportation as slaves to the galleys of the Mediterranean. The area took years to recover from the depopulation; indeed some villages have never recovered. As a result there are many that remain just as they were four centuries ago, time-locked in 16th-century France. A visit to these is fascinating, and any such trip goes through scenery that is equally interesting. The Pélicier Forest at the northeastern tip of the hills is planted with Austrian (black) pine, while the Petit Lubéron – as the smaller section of the range, lying to the west of Bonnieux, is known – has a forest of atlas cedar. The Petit Lubéron also has sections that are very wild and rocky, where Montpellier maple and wild lavender grow. Here, too, there are wild boar and beaver, while the sharp-eyed birdwatcher might catch a glimpse of an Egyptian vulture, a short-toed or a Bonelli's eagle or, for the very lucky (or very patient), an eagle owl.

**Vineyards cover the hillsides in the Rhône Valley**

**Fontaine-de-Vaucluse**

## ANSOUIS

*MAP REF: 112 C2*

Set on the southern flank of the Lubéron Hills, Ansouis would appear to have the ideal position for a village. It was not built to take advantage of its situation, however, but to service the great château of the Sabran family which dominates it. The château was originally built in the 11th century by the dukes of Forcalquier, but after 200 years it passed into the hands of the Sabrans, who have held it continuously for more than 600 years. Visitors are welcome (daily except Tuesdays) and will be impressed by the way the original fortifications seem to grow out of the bedrock. A link with the castle's early history is the fine collection of arms and armour.

Outside, the château's terrace offers a wonderful view of the vineyards and orchards of the Lubéron, of the Durance valley and, more locally, of the chestnut tree-lined avenue that completes the transformation from castle to country house.

An exploration of the village beside the castle should start at the place des Hôtes, from where narrow streets of mostly 17th- and 18th-century houses, built of golden Lubéron stone, lead off. For the most picturesque view find the rue Basse. At the top of the village is the place Haute, close to the town hall with its railed stairway. The belfry, with a fine ironwork bell cage, was once part of the medieval walls. Finally, a few minutes could be spent in the Georges Mazoyer Musée Extraordinaire.

## APT MARKET SAT A.

*MAP REF: 112 C3*

This small but busy town in the Calavon valley was originally a Roman settlement *(Apta Julia)* and it is claimed that the first Christian church in Gaul was built here in the 4th century. Below the present church are two ancient crypts, including the remains of the earliest church, and legend has it that the remains of St Anne, mother of the Virgin Mary, were placed here after being brought to Europe from the Holy Land. Because of this, Apt soon became a centre for pilgrimages, a tradition that has lasted for centuries. Anne of Austria is said to have sent treasures to the church following the birth of her son, the future Louis XIV. These treasures can still be seen in the old cathedral, an 11th-century building with excellent, but later, stained-glass windows. Those interested in Apt's early history will find a trip to the Archaeo-logical Museum rewarding, while a visit to the new Lubéron Museum will provide information on the Lubéron Regional Park.

Otherwise, Apt is a town to enjoy at leisure: the old, narrow alleys are crammed with interesting shops, and small squares offer numerous chances for rest and refreshment. Be sure to see the 16th-century clock tower, symbol of the town. And if your visit is on a Saturday, the weekly market is a showpiece for local craftworkers as well as for market garden produce.

**Nearby** Saignon is a perched village, set on a projecting ridge of the hills close to a prominent rock.

It offers excellent views towards Mont Ventoux and the Vaucluse Plateau, and the Romanesque church is worth visiting to see its beautiful arcading.

### CANDIED FRUIT

Apt is a famous centre for the production of candied and crystallised fruits, a process that started in the days before refrigeration and canning, but which today represents the luxury end of the fruit market. In principle all fruits can be candied, but the most commonly used are those with the strongest flavours – apricots, pineapple, cherries and so on – as the candying process tends to lessen the flavour. The process is simple: bring your fruits to the boil in plain water, simmer until tender and pour off the water/juice mixture. To this mixture sugar is added to make a syrup, and the fruit is then placed in the syrup. Part of the process takes days, the syrup being decanted, sugared again and repoured and, occasionally, the fruit/syrup mix being heated for long periods – hence the high cost of the end product. At last the fruit, now totally impregnated with sugar, is dried and finished off either by dusting with sugar (to produce crystallised fruit) or by dipping in boiling syrup to produce a glacé finish.

**The village of Ansouis clusters around its hill, dominated by the 11th-century château**

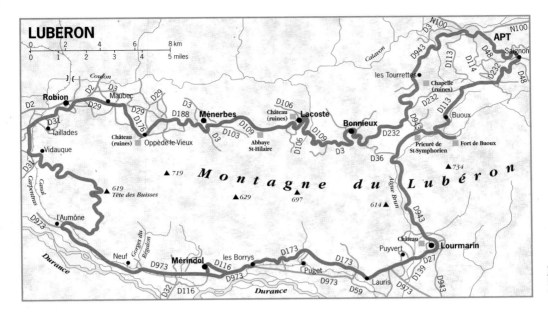

# MOTOR TOUR

This tour of just under 100km circuits the Petit Lubéron – or western half of the massif – to show both its forested and its wild and craggy aspects.

*Start in Apt.*

**Apt**
The office of the Parc Naturel Régional du Lubéron, at 1 place Jean-Jaurès can provide books, posters and maps of the area, and you can visit the Museum of Palaeontology. For walkers who want to learn more about the local environment, the Maison du Parc offers themed guided walks free of charge, but you must book beforehand. Wear strong shoes and take plenty of water in hot weather.

*Take the D943 southwest to Bonnieux, via Les Tourettes.*

**Bonnieux**
*En route* you pass several wine *domaines* and *caves*: in Bonnieux itself one of the best known is the Château de la Canorgue on route du Pont Julien. Bonnieux is a large village, charming and inevitably fashionable (see page 18), with an upper quarter around the old church and a Musée de la Boulangerie on rue de la République below. From Bonnieux you can follow the *Walking* signposted 'botanical footpath' into the Forêt des Cèdres, one of the most popular walking areas of Lubéron.

*Take the D109 to Lacoste, a perched village crowned by a castle.*

**Lacoste**
Privately owned and slowly being restored, the castle's most notorious period was in the mid-18th century, when it was owned by the Marquis de Sade. A charming village and supremely fashionable, it has nevertheless kept its authenticity.

*Continue to Ménerbes, passing a series of ancient quarries just outside Lacoste.*

**Ménerbes and Oppède-le-Vieux**
For a full description of Ménerbes and the next village, Oppède-le-Vieux, see page 26.

*From Oppède take the D176 to Maubec, a small village at the foot of the Lubéron which holds a Marché Paysan on Sunday* market *mornings and a music festival in June. Continue to Robion.*

**Robion**
This larger village also holds a renowned summer festival, with concerts and plays performed in the open-air theatre, while in neighbouring Taillardes, the August festivities are held in the enclosure formed by old stone quarries.

*Take the D31 south, turning left for Vidauque, then right to climb the scenic – and steep – road through the Forêt du Lubéron and past the Tête des Buisses peak. After dropping down from the Trou-du-Rat, turn left on to the D973.*

**Mérindol**
Mérindol has a tragic history. A Protestant stronghold for centuries, in the mid-16th century it was the target of a crusade launched by François I and executed by the local Baron of Oppède, slaughtering the inhabitants and then destroying the village itself.

*Leave the main road at Les Borrys to take the more scenic, but slower back road to Lauris. After the cemetery, bear left on the D27 in order to reach Lourmarin.*

**Lourmarin**
The elegant Renaissance château on the edge of the village is filled with eclectic treasures from Egypt, China, Spain and Provence, which you can see on a guided tour. The picturesque streets and splashing fountains make for pleasant strolling.

*Head north from the village to cross the Lubéron range through the Combe de Lourmarin, which follows the Aiguebrun torrent. After 8.5km, turn right for Buoux.*

**Buoux**
To the right you pass the slender and elegant tower rising from the ruins of the 12th-century St-Symphorien priory. The village of Buoux lies on the D113 to the left, but more interesting is a visit to the ruined Fort de Buoux – not to be confused with the Château de Buoux, a Renaissance castle now restored in part. The ruined fort, which you must reach on foot, stands on a rock pedestal – an important defensive site since prehistoric times, judging by the remains found over the extensive area.

*Return to Apt via the D232 and Saignon.*

# •AVIGNON•

**Though famous for the medieval bridge of the nursery rhyme song, and for a medieval period when it was the centre of European politics, Avignon has a history that goes back much further than those times. The site – a defensive one where the trade route rivers, the Rhône and Durance, meet – was occupied in the Bronze Age and saw both Celtic and Roman periods before becoming embroiled in the complicated politics of medieval Europe.**

That period in the city's history was responsible for the ramparts, which still remain intact, complete with 39 defensive towers. For the visitor Avignon (map ref: 112 B3) lies within these ramparts, a busy and interesting city that makes the modern town outside seem ordinary, even dull, by comparison. Within the old city the visitor will be drawn to Pont St- Bénézet to see the *pont d'Avignon* described in the well-known children's song *Sur le pont d'Avignon*. The bridge was built in 1190 and bears the name of a local shepherd boy. Time and floods have taken their toll, and today only about half the bridge remains - with a curious little chapel close to the bank. The nursery song's lyrics refer to a circling dance under *(sous)* - not on *(sur)* - the bridge. In fact, the dancing took place on an island beneath the bridge, the circle being made around one of the bridge piers.

From the bridge a steep but interesting climb through picturesque alleys leads to the place du Palais and Avignon's huge Palais des Popes (the Palace of the Popes), built in grand style in the 14th century. Externally the palace is imposing, with its turrets and battlements, some 50m tall, and the overall effect is a little severe. Inside, the extent of the palace becomes even more apparent, especially in the enormous Grand Hall, which is nearly 50m long and over 10m wide. The lack of furnishings merely adds to the majesty of the room. Elsewhere there are rooms that are elegantly decorated, the palace being a treasure house of medieval tapestries and paintings. Close to the palace is the Petit Palais, with a collection of medieval paintings and sculptures, while a little way south is the centre of Avignon's bustling modern street life, the place de l'Horloge.

Elsewhere in the old town,

Avignon has some fine museums, including the Musée Calvet, which houses a superb art collection. Another claim to fame is that here in the courtyard, in 1782, the Montgolfier brothers – who were born and raised in the rue St-Etienne close to the place de l'Horloge – carried out their earliest experiments with hot-air balloons.

**Nearby** Eastward from Avignon – about 6km along the N100, then off to the right on the N7F - is Montfavet, a village with a large 14th-century Gothic church. The church, once part of a monastery, has elegant, if massive, flying buttresses. South of Montfavet the village of Châteaurenard is also worth visiting to see the towers that guard the hill above it. These are all that remain of an early castle destroyed during the Revolution.

South of Avignon, the Abbaye de St-Michel-de-Frigolet is beautifully positioned. The name derives from the Provençal for thyme, for the abbey is set in a hollow of aromatic herbs. It is still a religious house, and the monks who live there sell a liqueur made from those herbs.

## TOWN WALK

This walk concentrates on the northwest quarter of the walled town, which itself makes up less than one quarter of the city as a whole.

*Start the walk from the Pont St-Bénézet.*

1 To visit the small St-Nicolas chapel – part Romanesque, part Gothic – which stands at the top of the four remaining arches of the celebrated bridge, climb up to the Castellet, the small fortress which was built in the 14th century to defend this lucrative thoroughfare (admission charge). Today it houses a branch of the local tourist office.

*Enter the walled city through the Porte du Rhône. Via rue Ferruce and the Balance quarter, climb the stepped rue Pente Rapide in order to reach the place du Palais.*

2 This vast expanse was still a choked maze of houses until the early 15th century. In addition to the mighty palace itself you can visit the Musée du Petit Palais at the northern end of the square (left), the Rocher des Doms park

and the cathedral of Notre-Dame des Doms.

*At the southeast corner of the square, between the palace and the Banque de France, take the left-hand street, rue Peyrollerie.*

3 Named for the coppersmiths who once worked in this area, the narrow street hugs the mighty walls of the palace and passes beneath a buttress supporting the Grande Chapelle – one of the few corners of Avignon where you can still imagine what the medieval city was like. The Roman arcades date from the 1st century, while opposite stands the 12th-century Palais de Commune.

*Continue to the place St-Pierre.*

4 From here you can make a detour north via rue Banasterie (street of the basketmakers), and the chapel of the Penitents Noirs. The chapel, built in 1739, has an ornate baroque façade. The church of St-Pierre dates from the 14th century and its flamboyant façade is dominated by a pair of enormous walnut doors, carved by Antoine Volard in 1551.

*Cross place Carnot behind the church and turn right on to rue des Marchands.*

5 As its name suggests, this was the old commercial heart of the city. At the corner with rue des Fourbisseurs look for the Hôtel de Rascas with its 15th-century

*auvent*, or roof canopy, while just before place de l'Horloge, rue du Change leads to the tiny place du Change, named for its medieval moneychangers, and the city's largest open space before the place du Palais was cleared in 1404. Place de l'Horloge, once the Roman city's forum, is now the centre of café life. A clock tower is all that remains of a medieval tower, adapted to a bell tower in the 15th century. The imposing Hôtel de Ville and Théâtre are both ornate 19th-century, but behind the Maison des Pays de Vaucluse (next to the theatre), the place Campana is a contemporary contrast, with modern bells designed by Roger Bezombes.

*From the southwest corner of the square, take rue St-Agricol.*

6 The Palais du Roure (just off the southern corner of the street near the statue of Mistral) is an elegant 15th-century mansion which now houses the Centre d'Etudes Méridionales. Rue St-Agricol has several interesting shops, including two popular ice-cream parlours and another of the city's main churches. Dedicated to Avignon's patron saint and dating from the 7th century, when he was bishop, it is mostly 14th- to 16th-century and the tower has recently been renovated.

*Continue to the junction with rue Joseph Vernet and turn right, opposite the 18th-century Chapelle de l'Oratoire.*

7 Here you will find some of Avignon's most exclusive and elegant shops. The local 18th-century painter for which the street is named is represented in the excellent Musée Calvet (follow rue Vernet south).

*Turn left at the junction with rue Folco de Baroncelli, next to a house with a small tower and Renaissance bull's eye window. Cross place Crillon.*

8 The façade is all that remains of Avignon's 18th-century theatre, La Comédie. Across from it stands the city's most elegant hotel – the Europe – which has been welcoming travellers since 1799. Bargain-hunters should visit place Crillon on Saturday mornings, when a *brocante* (second-hand goods) market is held here: other markets to look out for include a flea market in place des Carmes on Sunday mornings, a flower market in the same square on Saturdays and a large *brocante* fair on the Allée de l'Oulle in June.

*Continue north on rue Grand-Fusterie, which rejoins rue Ferruce.*

9 This and nearby rue Petite-Fusterie recall the time when this was the quarter of wood merchants. It has several imposing Renaissance mansions, including the 15th-century Hôtel de Tertulle at no 8 and, at no 29, the Gothic façade of the former Hôtellerie du Chapeau-Rouge.

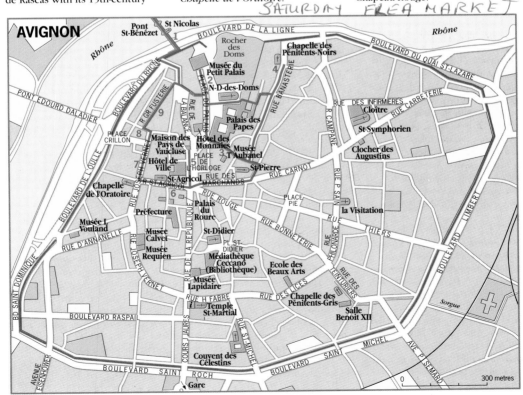

**Bollène, a typical Provençal town overlooking the Rhône**

## BEAUMES-DE-VENISE
*MAP REF: 112 B3*

Visitors to this terraced village – almost the last village on the southern flank of the foothills of the Dentelles, the sharp range of peaks west of Mont Ventoux – could be forgiven for wondering what possible connection there can be with the great Renaissance city of Venice. The answer is: none! The addition to the village's name reflects that this was Beaumes in the Comtat Venaissin, rather than one of several other Beaumes. In ancient times the site, backed by inhospitable peaks and close to the valley of the Ouvèze, was a desirable one, and was fortified. Today only the ruins of the old castle are left, adding a picturesque touch to a walk around the village's tight alleys.

Near by is the reminder of an even earlier age of conflict. The Chapelle de Notre-Dame d'Aubune is much admired for its tall, square belfry ornamented with three fluted pilasters and the carved decorations on each face. Some experts claim the chapel dates from the 12th century, but others believe it to be older, perhaps the 8th century or earlier. There is a legend that on the grey-rock plateau on which the chapel stands the army of Charles Martel, the 8th-century Frankish leader, defeated a force of Saracens, many of whom lie buried below. Some say the chapel was built in praise of victory, but others say it was destroyed by Martel to teach the locals a lesson for befriending the invaders.

## BOLLENE
*MAP REF: 112 B3*

Since the days when the pope resided at Avignon, this small town on the eastern bank of the Rhône has been an important local market. Today it is typically Provençal, with wide, well-shaded boulevards as well as a maze of narrow alleys, some leading to unexpected, delightful viewpoints. Once such is the Belvédère Pasteur, a small park dedicated to the memory of Louis Pasteur, who stayed in the town in 1882 while he was developing an effective inoculation against swine fever. Close by, the town museum includes several drawings by Picasso and Chagall and a collection of work by local artists. Another good view of the Rhône valley can be had from the town church, which stands on a convenient knoll.

## BONNIEUX
*MAP REF: 112 C3*

Bonnieux lies on the road that divides the Lubéron into its 'Petit' and 'Grand' sections, and when approached from the south the huddle of houses, church, and medieval rampart looks entrancing. In medieval times there were three ramparts, the walls having been pushed outward as the town grew. Sadly, as the town was Catholic when most of the area was Protestant, even three ramparts did not protect it. Over three-quarters of its 4,000 inhabitants were killed when it was attacked.

Bonnieux is a steep village, and stepped paths are occasionally needed between the beautiful old houses to reach the 12th-century church. From its cedar-shaded terrace the view to the Lubéron is breathtaking. One of the village's old buildings now houses a museum of baking, its rather unexpected, but fascinating, collection dealing with one of the simpler gastronomic pleasures of France – its bread.
**Nearby** Close to Bonnieux is Lacoste. Here, in the 12th century, there was an important abbey dedicated to St-Hilaire, of which only the chapel now remains. Rather more remains of the château, which was once the home of the infamous Donatien Alphonse François, better known as the Marquis de Sade. Sade spent only four years at the château – for which the village folk were doubtless grateful, as he was local lord of the manor for 30 years. Legend has it that several young people in the village were the victims of his perversions. The château has been partially restored. The village itself is of typically Provençal character, with narrow alleys which are occasionally bridged by attractive vaulted walkways.

## SYNAGOGUES

During the 14th century, when they were being persecuted throughout the country, the French Jewish community fled to the relative safety of the Comtat Venaissin, setting up synagogues in many of the local towns. Of these, the best-preserved is that in Carpentras; built in the early 15th century, when the town had a sizeable ghetto, it was greatly remodelled in the 18th century. The synagogue can be visited: there is an oven for baking unleavened bread, a fine collection of lamps and candlesticks, and a bath for full immersion, known in Provençal as the *cabussadou* (head first). Interestingly, Carpentras Cathedral has a Jewish door, through which Jewish converts to Christianity were led for baptism. Further information on the Jewish community in the Comtat can be found in the small museum which has been set up in the Cavaillon synagogue.

Sénanque, founded in 1148 and one of the 'Three Sisters of Provence', the other two being Thoronet and Silvacaine. Until about a hundred years ago the abbey could be reached only by mule track (even the present road is narrow and awkward), offering a remoteness in keeping with the austerity of the Cistercian order which held it. Dissolved at the time of the Revolution, it has now been re-established by the Cistercians, who are restoring it.

## L'ISLE-SUR-LA-SORGUE

*MAP REF: 112 B3*

In keeping with the local vogue for somewhat misleading nicknames, this small town has been called the 'Venice of Comtat' because here the River Sorgue divides into five branches which flow among the houses. At one time each tributary ran a mill, and a fine old waterwheel, gnarled and mossy, still stands in the town's public gardens. The rivers, with their plane-tree-shaded banks, are quiet places – though less so in July during the local festival, when night-time sees them covered with decorated floats as a prelude to a battle of flowers.

Whether arriving in July or not, visitors should see the town's baroque church to admire the wood panelling decorated in Italian style, and should visit the 18th-century hospital, which has a superb fountain in its courtyard – and a pharmacy displaying a fine range of Moustiers pottery jars.

### WINE

Vaucluse is famous for Châteauneuf-du-Pape, one of the great red wines of France, but there are several other wines that are also worth considering. Only in 1973 did the wines of the Côtes du Ventoux achieve AOC *(Appellation d'Origine Contrôlée)*, but today the Grenache of Gigondas, a strong and fruity red wine, is thought to be second only to Châteauneuf in terms of quality. Close to Gigondas is Beaumes-de-Venise, whose white Muscatel is excellent, if unfashionable.

The Lubéron is the other significant wine-producing area of Vaucluse, offering the full range of wines, well-balanced reds, delicate whites and delightfully crisp rosés.

**Châteauneuf-du-Pape**

### BORIES

A traditional Vaucluse peasant dwelling dating from Celtic times was the *borie*, a beehive-shaped hut built from slabs of stone laid in a continuous, dry-stone spiral – just as igloos are fashioned from ice blocks – and finished with a single slab across the spiral's neck. The construction sounds precarious, but in fact *bories* are remarkably sturdy, some having survived intact for centuries. On the Vaucluse Plateau, and especially around Gordes, *bories* will often be seen in fields, and about 4km from Gordes there is a whole village of them, grouped around a communal bread oven.

**Gigondas produces fine red wine**

23

*Handwritten notes:*

"COUSTELLET"
SUNDAY COUNTRY
MARKET

~~GORD~~ "GORDES"
MARKET TUES

UZÈS — MARKET
WED

CUCURON — MARKET
TUES

# ·MARKETS·

**Fresh fish for sale at Marseille's daily market**

You can find a market for practically every day of the week in Provence. And though they are infinite in their variety, there are some things that are sure to be there – stalls of dozens of different mixes of glistening olives, for instance, a van selling cheeses, another *charcuterie*. Then there will be the traditional Provençal printed fabrics in gaudy colours and, in contrast, the curious drab black, white and grey-patterned material designed for widows, which is made into old-fashioned pinafores.

## SIGHTS AND SMELLS

Many of the itinerant sellers go from one market to another, the hurdy-gurdy man, for instance, and the herb sellers who are on hand to advise you on what you need; special mixtures, camomile to calm you, *tilleul* (lime flower) to make you sleep. There are also soaps and creams made from lavender, linden and olive oil. Other stalls display delicious *confitures* and pickles. Another staple item is a mix of small fish labelled *soupe de poisson*. But besides the smell of spit-roasted chickens and the sounds of pop music, each market has a personality all its own. The larger markets in places like L'Isle-sur-la-Sorgue, for instance, have an exotic section where immigrants from North Africa sell their spices and specialities, with Arab music adding to the atmosphere.

Large places like Avignon, Nice, Cagnes, Grasse, Marseille and Ste-Maxime and, in the Vaucluse, Carpentras, have daily markets (though the flower market at Nice is closed on Monday). St-Rémy and St-Raphaël have daily markets as well; so do the Roman town of Vaison-la-Romaine and Vallauris, in pottery country.

Monday is a good day to go marketing, since the shops are shut in many places. Forcalquier, up in the hills, has its market then.

Cavaillon, centre of the melon industry, has a Monday market, too. It tends to concentrate on tools, kitchen equipment and clothes, but all the other shops in the town are open too. Nîmes' Monday market, an intriguing mix of flowers and antiques, is well worth a visit, and there's a flea market for bric-à-brac on Sunday.

## ANTIQUES

The most important antiques market in France, after Paris, is on Sundays at L'Isle-sur-la-Sorgue in the Vaucluse, though some antique stalls are also there on Saturdays. The whole town is now given over to antiques of all kinds, with the old train station housing almost a hundred shops. But there are plenty of bargains to be had among the bric-à-brac.

## FLEA MARKETS

The *marché aux puces*, the flea market, is a strong Provençal tradition. Here you will find not just antiques, ceramics and *objets d'art* but ancient fraying *boutis* (the traditional quilted bedcovers in old Provençal prints), heavy linen sheets monogrammed with the initials of former owners, and Provençal linen petticoats, too, which make wonderful simple sundresses or night-gowns.

Avignon has a fascinating Saturday flea market where you

can pick up all sorts of unusual treasures. There is also a flea market at Bormes-les-Mimosas every other Saturday in summer, and one at Draguignan on the first Saturday of every month. Toulon's bustling flea market is held on a Sunday, while Menton has one on Friday.

The thing to look out for in summer, if you are seriously interested in bric-à-brac, is the *Grande Braderie*, which is announced by posters nailed to trees in hill villages. The most amazing bargains can be found as the locals set up stalls to sell off what they consider to be outmoded family items. At St-Saturnin-d'Apt in the Vaucluse, the *mairie* sends out a form to all the local house-owners offering them a segment of pavement from which to sell their goods at the *Grande Braderie* on 14 July. Inevitably, professional dealers have now muscled in on sales such as these, but they are certainly still worth a visit, and the day often ends in a fête with hoop-la stalls, wine tastings and a local band.

## COUNTRY MARKETS

One of the best typical country markets is the one held at Apt in the Vaucluse on Saturday mornings. At one end it's a mixture of food and clothes and bric-à-brac, while up at the top of town you can buy plants from stalls laid out under the plane trees. Near by at Coustellet on Sundays there is a *marché paysanne,* where vegetables and plants rub elbows with antiques. A visit here could be combined with a trip to the market at L'Isle-sur-la-Sorgue.

There are also good country markets to be found at Digne, up in the mountains, on Wednesdays and Saturdays. Sault, an almost alpine town on the slopes of Mont Ventoux, has its market on Wednesday, when you can buy the local delicacy, wild boar pâté. And if you're looking for arts and crafts, go to picturesque Gordes which has its market on Tuesdays. Tuesday is also market day at Fontaine-de-Vaucluse, not far away, and at Tarascon, while red ochred Roussillon in the same area has its market day on Wednesday, as do Salon-de-Provence and Uzès. Others worth visiting include the Oppède market on Thursdays, and the one at Moustiers-Ste-Marie on Friday when you should be able to pick up pottery seconds.

On the tourist track, Stes-Maries-de-la-Mer in the Camargue has market days on Monday and Friday, where you are likely to see gypsies mingling with the local *gardians,* or cowboys. And there are markets at St-Tropez on Tuesday and Saturday. Saturday is market day in a number of other towns, including Aix-en-Provence, Arles, Manosque, Fréjus and Brignoles.

## SPECIALITIES

France also has a number of specialised markets at certain times of year. The big old-fashioned daily market at Carpentras changes through the year as specialities come in. In May there are stalls laden with cherries, in the autumn, grapes. During the winter it is the place to come for truffles and locally shot game.

If you are fond of asparagus, Le Thor, between Avignon and L'Isle-sur-la-Sorgue, has an asparagus market on Saturdays through April and in May there is an asparagus market too at Pernes-les-Fontaines and at Bonnieux. Le Barroux has an apricot market throughout the week from late July to the end of August, while melons and grapes are a speciality on Tuesdays at the market of Cucuron from the beginning of August right through to November.

Digne, capital of the lavender country, has a lavender market from towards the end of August to the first week in September, when the crop has been cut. Those searching for 'black gold' should visit the truffle market at Riez, open Wednesdays and Saturdays from the middle of November to the end of March. Finally, don't miss the *santons* market in Marseille through December, when figures for Christmas cribs are sold. If you're planning to visit one of these places, bear in mind that market day is also traffic day, and to be sure of parking you need to be there around 8.30am. Most markets begin to pack up at noon.

**A colourful display at the Saturday market in Aix-en-Provence**

## MENERBES
### MAP REF: 112 C3

In the 16th century, France, particularly southern France, was torn apart by the Wars of Religion. The worst fighting was in the Massif Central, but the conflicts in the Lubéron Hills were also frequent and bloody. There were long sieges, one of which took place for control of Ménerbes, a village occupied by Protestants, which stands on a rocky spur at the northwestern extremity of the Lubéron.

Today Ménerbes is a strange place, still partially in ruins and, as a result, having several interesting spots, such as the medieval castle, that are difficult to reach. The upper section of the village – the older, ruinous section with its maze of narrow twisting alleys – is typically Provençal, and it was from here that the village folk resisted a 15-month siege, eventually fleeing to Switzerland in 1578. The castle is too dangerous to visit, but from close quarters some of the violence and determination of that time can be imagined. Ménerbes, which seems to grow out of the hillside, had the advantage of just one entrance and a spring within its walls. Finally, but unknown to those laying siege, there was a tunnel to the outside world along which the villagers travelled to bring in food.

This passage can still be traced (it ran northwards from the town hall) but has collapsed in several places and should not be entered.

The village church is in a better state of repair than the castle, but is frequently locked. If you are lucky enough to enter, be sure to look for the 'stained-glass windows' that are not as they seem, being very well executed murals rather than the genuine article.

## OPPEDE-LE-VIEUX
MARKET THURS
### MAP REF: 112 C3

The most westerly village on the Petit Lubéron is Oppède-le-Vieux, the addition on the name distinguishing it from the hill village, Les Poulivets-d'Oppède, at the base of the hill. As with all Lubéron villages, Oppède suffered in the Wars of Religion, but the conflict here was even crueller than elsewhere because Baron Oppède, the feudal lord, was Catholic while the villagers were Protestant. The baron attacked his own village, and after his victory sent hundreds of his own folk to Marseille as galley slaves. The village numbers never recovered, and Oppède was finally abandoned altogether at the end of the last century. Only relatively recently has it been rediscovered, and even now not all of the houses are renovated. As a result the

**Oppède-le-Vieux has never fully recovered from its ordeal during the Wars of Religion, when villagers were attacked by their lord**

village seems frozen in time, a preserved piece of medieval France. The church may be closed, and the castle a dangerous ruin, but the village is sheer poetry.

## ORANGE
### MAP REF: 112 B3

When the Romans came this way in the 1st century BC, the town was *Arausio,* the local Celtic capital. The Romans took revenge on the town for the deaths of many legionaries several years before, and so complete was their vengeance that the site could later be totally taken over by veterans of the Second Legion: they turned it into a Roman town, complete with theatre, gymnasium and triumphal arch.

Much later, when France gave the Comtat Venaissin to Rome, the town was excluded from the gift, and it eventually passed to William the Silent, Prince of Orange and founder of Holland. It is from the prince that the town's name is derived, as William's son, Maurice of Nassau, moved here in 1622. The name has also passed to South Africa's Orange Free State and to several other places. Ironically, the citrus fruit of the same name is not apparently associated either with the town or with its prince, though many visitors may assume it is!

Maurice of Nassau fortified Orange, and it is purely as a result of this that the Roman theatre has survived, the huge façade wall of red sandstone having been incorporated into the defences. The wall, said Louis XIV, was 'the finest wall in my kingdom'. The theatre of which it formed a part was built into the hill of Colline St-Eutrope, which can be climbed for a superb panorama of Orange and the Rhône valley (the modern-looking complex is the Marcoule nuclear power centre). From the tiered amphitheatre of seats the audience looked down on the stage side of Louis' finest wall, a 103m by 36m structure comprising 76 columns, numerous frescos and niches with statues. Only one statue remains, a carefully restored 3.5m-high rendering of Emperor Augustus, complete with baton. On the stage below, you can still see the supports for poles which held awnings to protect the players from sun and rain. The guided tour of the site also looks at some of the stage machinery, which has survived not only the rigours of time but also the use of the theatre as a handy quarry by the townsfolk of Orange. The theatre is still in use; up to 10,000 spectators watch plays and an international music festival in late July. The acoustics are said to be superb.

Orange's gymnasium, beside the theatre, is the sole surviving structure of its kind in Roman Gaul, an enormous site almost 400m long and 80m wide. It comprised a temple, baths and athletics track, with a raised platform at one end for gladiatorial contests. The best finds from here, and from the theatre, can be seen in the town museum. One of the most interesting relics is a marble slab carved with a plan of Roman Orange, with shop- and home-owners' names, and their tax rates, shown. The final Roman remain of note is the superb triple arch that commemorates the taking of the area. It is complete with naked, hairy Gauls being vanquished or in chains, the Roman architect being a little tactless when it came to portraying the locals. Once the arch stood on the Via Agrippa, the major route along the Rhône valley, leading to Lyon. This road was later followed by the N7. In fact, with the building of the A7 autoroute, Orange was bypassed for the first time in 2,000 years.

For visitors seeking respite from the Romans, the old cathedral is a fine 12th-century Romanesque building, while Orange itself is a lively town with a good assortment of shops and cafés.

## PERNES-LES-FONTAINES

*MAP REF: 112 B3*

Pernes is another town that was once the capital of the Comtat Venaissin. Although no longer so important, it is still a thriving market for locally grown fruit, especially cherries and strawberries. Part of the medieval rampart is still intact, and is best seen close to the old bridge over the River Nesque, a bridge that preserves a tiny chapel built on it in the 16th century. Close to the bridge the Notre-Dame gate still leads through the old walls into the town. Here, too, is the keep of the old town castle, built by the Counts of Toulouse. Another, older tower – the Tour de Ferrande, dating from the 12th century – is open to the public and is worth visiting for the 13th-century frescos and the view it offers of the town.

**Nearby** From Orange an essential excursion for the naturalist is to the village of Sérignan-du-Comtat, where the entomologist Jean-Henri Fabre (1823–1915) lived and where his home, L'Harmas, houses a collection on local natural history as well as his desk and laboratory. Fabre moved to Sérignan in 1879 and lived there until his death. Known as the 'Homer of the Insects' – yet another Vauclusian nickname – he is best remembered for his work on Vaucluse insects, which he described in an intimate, elegant style. During his life other scientists often ignored him because of his 'crime' of dismissing Darwin's theories, but modern scientists tend to view him rather more generously. The great man is buried in Sérignan's cemetery, and a statue of him graces the village square.

**A detail in the well preserved Roman theatre in Orange**

predates all of these, dating from the 11th century. Interestingly, the village has both a church and a chapel; the latter is by far the more interesting, a fine 12th-century Romanesque building set among cypress trees. From the chapel, which is dedicated to St Saturnin, the views of the Lubéron Hills, the Coulon valley and the Vaucluse Plateau are exquisite.

The village church is surprisingly recent, having been built in the 19th century in neo-classical style. Equally surprising is the fact that it is dedicated to St-Etienne rather than St-Saturnin, the village's saint. Inside there is a very beautiful 15th-century wooden pietà.

*Make Nougat*

## SAULT  *MARKET WED:*
### MAP REF: 112 C3

Sault must lay claim to being the loveliest-smelling village in Provence when, in July, the local lavender fields are in full bloom. From these huge fields waves of the sweet scent of lavender descend upon the village, adding a rare piquancy to a coffee at one of the pavement cafés. The lavender is distilled in local factories for the perfume industry.

Another local industry, more cottage than factory, is the making of nougat. For most visitors to the

*MARKET WED:*

## ROUSSILLON
### MAP REF: 112 C3

Most unusually, Roussillon's name is derived from the colour of the houses and the underlying rock of the surrounding land. This area of the Vaucluse Plateau is famous for its ochre rock, and the village – set high on the ochre hills that form a ridge between the Coulon valley and the plateau proper – is built of this rock, the house walls and roofs comprising dozens of different colours. Any clambering walk through the network of narrow streets is a delight, as the colours change spectacularly, but the rue de l'Arcade is a must: it ends at a wonderful viewpoint, a panoramic dial pointing out details of the plateau, the Coulon valley and the Lubéron Hills. At the other end of the village, another vantage point allows a view of the Aiguilles du Val des Fées (the Needles of the Valley of Fairies), a series of curious, jagged rocks. Southeast of the village a short walk leads to a viewpoint of the Chaussée des Géants, (the Giant's Causeway), an array of rust-red cliffs. South again, the River Coulon is spanned by the Pont Julien, widely held to be the best-preserved Roman bridge in France. Though named for Julius Caesar, who established a colony locally, the bridge was actually built in the 1st century AD, and carried the Via Domitia, one of Provence's most important roads. The odd-looking extra 'arches' in the structure were designed, and successfully so, to allow the flood waters of the Coulon to pass without damaging the structure.

**Weathered ochre rock: its rich, gold-red colour gave the village of Roussillon its name and adds to an atmospheric setting**

## RUSTREL
### MAP REF: 112 C3

Even more spectacularly colourful than Roussillon are the huge ochre quarries of the Rustrel Colorado, a little way east of St-Saturnin-d'Apt. The Colorado must be approached on foot: leave your car at the convenient park beside the River Doa, cross the stream and follow the path, allowing about two hours for the return journey. Some of the quarries are still working, but the trip is quite safe; do, however, keep an eye on children, as some of the older quarries included underground workings. Alternatively, a fine viewpoint is reached off the D22 to the west of the village of Bouvène. The most impressive part of the trip is a view of the 'mushrooms' created by pillars of ochre topped by clay caps.

## ST-SATURNIN-D'APT
### MAP REF: 112 C3

Once, this delightful little village was heavily fortified, as befitted its strategic position on the edge of the Vaucluse Plateau. Few reminders of that time remain now, but those that do are of great interest. The Porte Ayguier is the oldest remnant of those times, built in 1420 as a gateway through the walls. Later, the clock tower and Tour du Portalet were added. The castle, now sadly in ruins,

South of France, nougat means Montelimar, but the Boyer family of Sault claim to be the only makers of real nougat. Nougat (the word means 'almond-flavoured') is a Provençal speciality, which was once eaten only at Christmas and New Year. Today the Boyer family make nougat for all-year consumption and, though the basis is honey, egg white and almonds, the precise ingredients are kept secret.

In days gone by the honey probably came from the Rocher du Cire (the Rock of Wax), set in the Gorges de la Nesque to the south west of Sault. This remarkable cliff, almost 300m high and honeycombed with caves, has for generations attracted wild bees whose outpourings of wax have given the rock its curious lustre. The rock was known to Frédéric Mistral, the Nobel Prize-winning poet who wrote in the Provençal language; lines from one poem in which he mentioned the rock are etched into a tablet at the viewpoint in the Nesque Gorge.

Back in Sault is the 12th-century church with its beautiful columned nave, while the museum, housed in the library building, has fine collections of local archaeological finds and an exhibit on the region's geology.

## SEGURET

*MAP REF: 112 B3*

The vineyards that grow on the southern slopes of the Dentelles de Montmirail produce wines that have only recently been granted an AOC. The wine production – chiefly red, but with some rosé and a little white – is concentrated in a small number of villages close to the base of the hills. One of the best of these villages is Séguret. Normally in Provence the villages that are claimed to be the most beautiful are the perched villages. Séguret is an exception to that rule. Set against a rocky hillside rather than on a rocky pinnacle, it is every bit as picturesque as the more famous hill villages. Lately its qualities have been recognised and it has become more popular with artists and visitors, but it is still a quiet place, good for a relaxing afternoon in gentle surroundings. Chief among the attractions for those intent on a little exploration are the 12th-century Porte Reynier, one of the last remnants of the village's medieval fortifications, and the village church, dating from around the same time. The church, which has a delightful little square bell tower, is the setting for a famous mystery play on Christmas Eve each year.

At that time it is also decorated with a Nativity scene made up of *santons* (the traditional Provençal clay figurines) and decorated by local artists and craftworkers. Those particularly interested in the figures may wish to time their visit with the village's *santon* exhibitions, which are held twice yearly, around Christmas and in July. Exhibitions and fairs seem to be popular in Séguret; there is also an annual display of local folklore throughout the summer months, and a Provençal festival in August.

Elsewhere in the village there are delightful little discoveries to be made in the steep, cobbled streets, some with vaulted passages. Two further medieval gates can be found – Porte de la Bise to the north and Port Neuf to the south – though the old ramparts can only be traced in the street geography. The ancient castle is in ruins, but these formidable gates give a clue to the village's name: in Provençal *ségur* means sure. Finally, there is that paradox of Provence: a bubbling fountain in an arid landscape. For good measure the Mascarons Fountain, erected in the 15th century, is beautiful.

**Sault, known for its lavender fields and its nougat**

# •VAISON-LA-ROMAINE•

**A century ago Baedeker's guide to Provence did not mention Vaison; its fame arose only when excavations of the old Roman site revealed the most complete town yet discovered in France. The remains do not have the immediate visual appeal of Orange's theatre or the amphitheatres of Arles and Nîmes, but are of considerable interest for the light they shed on the way of life of the ordinary citizen of the Roman Empire.**

In September 1992 the semi-swollen Ouvèze burst its banks, flooding Vaison (map ref: 112 B3) and causing the deaths of over 30 people in one of the worst natural disasters ever to have occurred in the Vaucluse. The cathedral and the Roman remains of the Villasse quarter were damaged: the cathedral was quickly restored and re-opened, but La Villasse will not open until late 1993, and some damage may be permanent.

Remarkably, the Pont Romain survived. The remains were divided into two areas, the second being the *quartier* of Puymin. Roman Vaison was constructed on an earlier Celtic site in the early 1st century AD by men of wealth and taste. The town soon became one of the richest in Provence and remained so until it was destroyed by the Franks in the 5th century. The remains of the Puymin quarter reflect the wealth and

sophistication of the settlers. What is known as Messius' House was a spacious villa with a water cistern, baths, lavatories, ovens and a sink. It was here that a head of Venus, one of the finest excavated remains, was found. The owner of the villa would have stepped out into a walled public promenade, elegantly paved and columned, its walls decorated with murals. Close by there was a public garden with a fine marble statue (now exhibited in the British Museum). He could have crossed the promenade to visit the theatre, which was smaller than that at Orange, but built to the same basic design – a semicircle set into the hillside – and was reached by a tunnel excavated from the central promenade. The Puymin quarter also includes the excavated remains of the town's piped water system, and a museum.

Close to the Villasse quarter, which includes the remains of shops and other villas, is the town's old cathedral, built in the 12th century, but on the foundations of an earlier Merovingian church, itself built only a hundred years or so after the Romans had been ejected. The first bishop of Vaison, St Quenin, who was born in the town and held office until 575, lies buried in a sarcophagus in front of the bishop's throne. The throne stands behind the altar in a superb vaulted and arcaded apse. Outside the cathedral there are the fine remains of a cloister.

The upper, medieval town is a more intimate place that is well worth exploring and should be visited on foot. It lies across Pont Romain, built in the 2nd century but repaired several times since. Access to this older quarter is through an arched gateway, a remnant of the medieval walls. Although it is not readily visible from the town, there is a ruined castle on the hill above. The castle was built during the 12th century, but it is now in a very sorry state and is closed to visitors. It can be approached, however, and even from its base there are excellent views stretching out across the Ouvèze valley and to Mont Ventoux.

In the town below the castle the visitor should enjoy wandering the streets at random: Vaison is an exquisite place, a close huddle of beautiful houses set in tight, steep streets. The wrought-iron work of later centuries adds to its picturesque qualities, as do the hanging baskets, alive with colour. Perhaps the highlight is the place du Vieux-Marché with its fountain.

# TOWN WALK

Although the Roman excavations are the obvious highlight of a visit to Vaison, it is well worth exploring the rest of this small town, in particular the medieval *Haute Ville* across the river. Assuming that you have already visited the *fouilles* (excavations), allow one to two hours for the walk suggested below.

*Start from the tourist office on place Abbé-Sautel, between the two extensive areas of Roman remains.*

1 Vaison's Maison du Tourisme is a particularly fine example of that historic French institution otherwise known as the *syndicat d'initiative*. Independent travellers who are planning several days in the *pays Voconce* can obtain information from here on everything from where to hire a bicycle to suggested wine tours or

the nearest golf course, as well as picking up useful leaflets on Vaison itself. The Maison du Vin which has an outlet here sells liqueurs, honey and, of course, wine, and occasionally organises *dégustations*.

*Cut across place du 11-Novembre in front of the post office and turn right into rue Trogue Pompée which leads along the southern side of the Villasse quarter. Continue up the footpath (chemin du Couradou) and turn left at the end to reach the former cathedral of Notre-Dame-de-Nazareth.*

2 If you have bought a 'global' ticket (valid for five days) for the Roman sites, it is also valid for the tiny Romanesque cloister behind the cathedral – a peaceful, completely restored Romanesque quadrangle with simple carvings and a small lapidary museum. The cathedral itself is stark Romanesque, constructed over a 6th-century Gallo-Roman basilica, parts of which can still clearly be seen together with fragments from other local Roman monuments. Inside you can see the octagonal cupola and two Roman marble altars. The cathedral fell into disrepair during the Hundred Years' War when the population moved to the protection of the fortress in the *Haute Ville* and a new church was built, which was restored in the 19th century.

*Cross the small gardens, turn left on to avenue Jules Ferry and then right on to quai Pasteur, passing a car park next to the*

river before reaching the Pont Romain (Roman bridge).

3 For those who like statistics, the solid single span bridge across the Ouvèze is 17m high and 9m wide. Only the parapet is said to have needed repair in the past 2,000 years – in 1616 after a flood and in 1944 when the bridge was mined.

*Turn right, cross the road (without a pavement) and begin the steep climb to the Haute Ville.*

4 The road passes under a fortified gateway topped by a clock tower and climbs up to rue de l'Evéché. The popular Hostellerie du Beffroi is a fascinating building from whose terrace you can enjoy views back over Vaison, while on summer Sunday mornings you can shop at the Provençal market around the fountain of place du Vieux-Marché. The street known as *la Juiverie* was the medieval Jewish quarter, typical in towns of the Comtat Venaissin. A path from rue des Fours climbs steeply to the abandoned fortress (not open) from where you are rewarded with a superb view, while down below you can catch your breath in the shady square in front of the church, from whose terrace there are more views upstream.

*Leave the Haute Ville and re-cross the Roman bridge, continuing up the main shopping street of Grande Rue to return to the town centre.*

**A glimpse of life in the Roman Empire: Vaison-la-Romaine's 1st-century theatre**

# •ROMAN PROVENCE•

In 124BC the Phocaeans, under attack from the Celts, asked the Romans for help. The Romans responded, but went further than the Phocaeans had intended. For the 'helpers' came, saw and conquered the whole of Provence, making it the first Roman province outside Italy. One of the first places to come under their protection was the important Phocaean port of *Massalia*, known now as Marseille. Part of the original Roman quayside, together with timbers from a Roman ship and olive jars, can be seen today in the Musée des Docks Romains in the city.

## ARRIVAL

When the Romans arrived, the region was inhabited by many tribes, the most important of which formed a confederation called the Salluvian Celts. They were defeated by Romans in 123BC at a bloody battle at Entremont. Sextius, the Roman consul concerned, decided to set up camp by a thermal spring some 3km away, founding the first Roman settlement in Provence. He called it *Aquae Sextiae* – today's Aix-en-Provence, and that same thermal spring now forms the fountain in the cours Mirabeau.

## POWER STRUGGLES

From its early days as *Massalia*, Marseille has had a long history of backing the wrong side in war. In 49BC, it backed Pompey in his rebellion against Julius Caesar (Pompey was killed in battle in 48BC). In revenge, Julius Caesar decided to set up a rival port to *Massalia* along the coast to take away its trade.

He put in a small garrison and built a new port called *Forum Julii*. Today it is known as Fréjus. Later Augustus turned it into an important naval base. At its peak it housed up to 400 war galleys, and it was from here, in 31BC, that ships set out to take part in the battle of Actium. As *Forum Julii* was not sited directly on the coast, a canal had to be built to connect it to the Mediterranean. The entrance was guarded by a powerful light known as Augustus' Lantern, which can still be seen among the ruins of the Roman citadel. Today, the best-preserved ruins in Fréjus are the aqueduct and the arena.

*Forum Julii* became the head-quarters of the important 8th Legion, and many Roman families settled there, making it a large city with twice as many inhabitants as present-day Fréjus. One of its celebrated sons was the emperor Agricola, who went on to conquer Britain.

## HOME FROM HOME

The Romans so enjoyed the South of France (or Gaul, as it was known) that they stayed there for

## AIX-EN-PROVENCE MARKET SAT

Aix is the antithesis of its southerly neighbour: compact and elegant, with a procession of fountains stretching out under the shady canopy of the broad cours Mirabeau. Cézanne lived and worked here, as did many lesser-known artists. The building housing the foundation dedicated to Victor Vasarély lies to the west of town, and Picasso is buried 14km to the east. Van Gogh, the other great artist of Provence, adopted the region as his home, moving first to Arles and then to St-Rémy, where he was treated at the hospital of St-Paul-de-Mausole.

## ST-REMY DAILY MARKET

St-Rémy is a pretty, historic, small town, birthplace of the astrologer Nostradamus and close to the impressive remains of the Roman town of *Glanum*. To the south rise the jagged limestone hills of the Alpilles and village of Les Baux, whose ruined castle once resounded to the strains of troubadours and courtly love.

To help you discover the region in more depth, we suggest walks around the historic hearts of the four main towns and a motor tour in the Alpilles hills to explore this part of historic Provence off the beaten track.

37

**Above: Arles – a fountain in the place de la République**

**Below: A detail from the mausoleum in *Glanum*, St-Rémy**

# •AIX-EN-PROVENCE•

An elegant, small, restrained city of soothing fountains, Aix is the perfect foil to the uncontrolled noise and bustle of Marseille, less than 30km away. Its grand mansions and tiny squares – part of a cultural and architectural legacy from centuries as the capital of Provence – combine with a lively summer arts festival and animated café-life to create perhaps the archetypal Provençal town, and certainly the favourite place of many first-time visitors to the region.

Hôtel de Ville, Aix-en-Provence

Like other towns in southern France such as Pau, Toulouse and Montpellier, Aix (map ref: 112 C2) has capitalised on qualities such as its environment and a long-established university to attract new high-tech businesses to locate here. But despite a population approaching 250,000, the heart of the town remains an intimate place, ideal to explore on foot.

The town's grandest thoroughfare, the cours Mirabeau, was laid out in the 17th century amid a flurry of construction that included public buildings such as the beautiful Hôtel de Ville and private *hôtels particuliers* in the new Quartier Mazarin, which lies to its south.

From the cathedral of St-Sauveur, signs direct you to the Atelier Paul Cézanne (cross boulevard Jean-Jaurès and take avenue Paul-Cézanne off avenue Pasteur), left largely as it would have been at the time of the artist's death in 1906. Just outside the boulevards that ring the town centre, the elegant Pavillon de Vendôme, with its beautiful gardens, was built for the Cardinal de Vendôme and is open to the public. It stands next to the Thermes Sextius (still in operation today) on rue de la Molle.

**For history buffs** The life and works of Nobel prize-winning poet St-John Perse (1887–1975) are documented with photographs and manuscripts in a small museum housed in the Hôtel de Ville. Scholars can also request to visit the extensive library of ancient books and manuscripts, which were collected by the Marquis de Méjanes in the 18th century.

If you have visited the Musée Granet (see page 39) and want to know more about the Oppidum d'Entremont – the Celtic-Ligurian settlement pre-dating the Roman town – take the D14 (avenue Pasteur) north of Aix for 2km to the Plateau d'Entremont. Though only the outline of the settlement remains, its natural defensive position is still obvious, with an excellent panorama to be had from the viewing table.

**Back to nature** To escape Aix as Cézanne did, head to the Montagne Ste-Victoire, a range of hills east of the city. The highest peak, marked by the monumental Croix de Provence, can be reached by a path from the the D17, which skirts the southern side of the ridge, or the D10, which runs around the north side. Some way further along the D10, Vauvernargues is the 17th-century château where Pablo Picasso spent the final years of his life; he is buried in the grounds (closed to the public).

**Nearby** Four kilometres west of town, at the Jas de Bouffan, the black and white circles and cubes of the Fondation Vasarély are a foretaste of the art inside. Besides its academic role, the foundation has an extensive display of Victor Vasarély's bold experiments with colour and illusion.

## AN HISTORIC CITY

The name Aix is derived from *Aquae Sextiae*, the name given by the Romans to their first settlement in Gaul – the 'waters (or spa) of Sextius', the conquering Roman consul. In the age of the troubadour, the court of the Counts of Provence at Aix flourished, culminating in the 15th century with the reign of King René –a remarkable scholar and patron of the arts remembered for, among other things, his encouragement of the cultivation of the muscat grape.

# TOWN WALK

*Start at the cours Mirabeau.*

**1** Though not quite the geographic heart of things, the great canopy of plane trees along the cours Mirabeau certainly marks the centre of activity in Aix. Here are some of the finest fountains, including the powerful jets of the Fontaine-Grande on the place Général de Gaulle and the gentle dribble of the mossy Fontaine d'Eau Thermale, the same warm mineral water which first attracted the Romans. Opposite the cafés are sombre *hôtels*, or mansions, several of which have elaborate doorways and wrought-iron balconies: look out in particular for the two giants who are guarding no 38.

*Opposite the Fontaine d'Eau Thermale take rue Clemenceau to the place St-Honoré. Turn left into place d'Albertas, then follow rue Aude to the right, which becomes rue Maréchal Foch.*

**2** On the right, two squares are separated by the former corn exchange, now a PTT (post office). The first, place Richelme, is the site of the daily vegetable market; the second, place de l'Hôtel de Ville, has the flower market. Opposite stands one of Aix's most beautiful buildings – the 17th-century Hôtel de Ville.

*Continue up rue Gaston de Saporta.*

**3** The Musée du Vieil Aix, in a fine 17th-century mansion, concentrates on local festivals and traditional crafts and has a good collection of old *santons*, clay figures originally made to represent the figures of the Nativity. Past the Fontaine d'Epéluque in place des Martyrs-de-la-Résistance and opposite place de l'Université on the left, is St-Sauveur Cathedral, a mix of ages and styles, with an octagonal baptistery dating back to 5th-century Roman Aix. In the Gothic aisle is the triptych painted by Nicholas Froment for King René in 1475 – the *Buisson Ardent* or the *Burning Bush.* The painting is kept locked up but can be seen on request. Also worth seeing are the carved panels on the west doors and, through the south door, the small, intricately carved Romanesque cloister. Fine tapestries can be seen in the Musée des Tapisseries, housed in the former Archbishop's Palace.

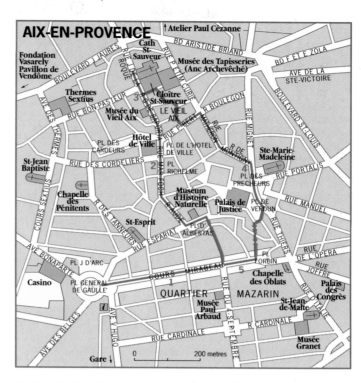

Head south from the square to rue Paul-Bert, turn left and then right into rue Matheron. Bear left after the fountain through rue de Montigny to place des Prêcheurs.

**4** The city's other main market-place is dominated by the Church of Ste-Marie-Madeleine, a 17th-century church behind its 19th-century façade. Its fine works of art include a marble statue of the Virgin by Chastel and a 15th-century triptych of the Annunciation (only the central panel remains). On place de Verdun, opposite, the Palais de Justice was rebuilt in its present neo-classical form on the site of the former castle of the Counts of Provence.

*From the southern corner of the place, take the covered passage*

Agard, which rejoins the cours Mirabeau near the Fontaine du Roi René.

**5** Aix's two fine arts museums are south of the cours in the Quartier Mazarin: the Musée Paul Arbaud on rue du 4-Septembre, where regional literature, porcelain and fine art are displayed; and the excellent Musée Granet in the former Commandery of the Knights of Malta, at the end of rue Cardinale. Works include a good collection of local artists. In the basement archaeological section are remains from Roman *Aquae Sextiae* and excavations at nearby Entremont. Next to the museum, the church of St-Jean-de-Malte was the chapel of the Knights of Malta.

**The Fontaine-Grande on the place Général de Gaulle**

40

## AIGUES-MORTES
### MAP REF: 112 A2

The 'Dead Water' that once lapped at the walls of this remarkable small town to the west of the Camargue has long since retreated. Though it hardly seems a name inspired to attract settlers, that was indeed the aim of Louis IX (St Louis) when he built the only French port in the Mediterranean in the 13th century. By 1248 Aigues-Mortes was ready for the departure of the Seventh Crusade, but Louis was not to survive the Eighth. He died in 1270, leaving the 15 towers and 10 gates of the town to be completed by his son, Philip the Bold.

Over 700 years later the town has hardly spread beyond those imposing walls. For the best view, stretching from salt marshes to the mountains, climb the Tour de Constance to the right of the main gateway, the Porte de la Gardette, from where you can also make a circuit of the ramparts. During the Wars of Religion the massive tower had a more grisly role as a prison; among the many

Louis IX watches over his creation, Aigues-Mortes, from the place St-Louis

Huguenots imprisoned here was Marie Durand, who endured 38 years of captivity.

The Grand Rue Jean-Jaurès leads to the pretty, shady place St-Louis, where a statue of the king surveys the church of Notre-Dame-des-Sablons, the Hôtel de Ville and the Cloître des Capucins, now the tourist information centre.
**Nearby** The sea has been replaced by expanses of salt marshes around Aigues-Mortes, and at Les-Salins-du-Midi the processes of large-scale salt extraction can be seen. Further southwest along the D979, Le Grau-du-Roi is a small fishing village popular with visitors for its waterside restaurants. On either side along the coast are new resorts – to the south the large marina of Port-Camargue and to the north the great modern ziggurats of La Grande Motte.

## ALPILLES, LES
### MAP REF: 112 B2

Northeast of Arles, seemingly endless horizons end abruptly in a series of limestone peaks, the Chaîne des Alpilles, dividing the Crau plain into la Crau to the south and la Petite Crau to the north. Though by no means mountainous, the contorted, stark white rock, surrounded by olive trees and fruit orchards makes for stunning scenery easily accessible by car, and at its centre is one of Provence's most famous villages – Les Baux (see page 46).

**A shop in Aigues-Mortes**

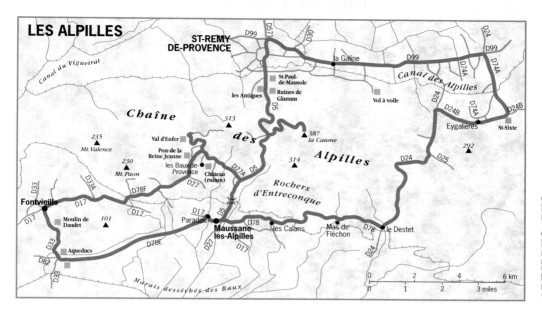

**LES ALPILLES**

## MOTOR TOUR

This motor tour of 65km starts from St-Rémy-de-Provence, but for those approaching from Arles could also begin from Fontvieille. Serious walkers can take on the length of the Alpilles chain by following the GR6 footpath.

*Leave St-Rémy (see page 56) south on the D5. After the Monastery of St-Paul-de-Mausole and the two Roman monuments called Les Antiques, the road climbs into the heart of the chain of hills, with superb views.*

### La Caume
For a complete panorama, turn off left to La Caume, the highest point, where the view stretches as far as the Camargue and Mont Ventoux.

*The D5 crosses the peak and descends towards the valley. Turn off right on to the D27A to Les Baux. After a detour north on the D27 to the Val d'Enfer (Devil's Valley), continue south on the D27 and D78F as far as the D17. Turn right for Fontvieille.*

### Fontvieille
Follow the avenue des Moulins (D33) south of the town to reach the Moulin de Daudet (windmill) – the inspiration for (but not where Alphonse Daudet actually wrote) his *Lettres de Mon Moulin* – with a small museum and a memorable view. The nearby Château de Montauban, home of the Ambroy family, where Daudet often stayed, has another museum dedicated to the author, which you can visit on a joint ticket with the Moulin de Daudet.

*Continue south to the crossroads with the D82 and turn left.*

### Aqueducs de Barbegal
A short walk on either side of the road reveals the ruins of the Roman Aqueducs de Barbegal, built to supply Arles with water from Eygalières. Another branch supplied a large flour mill, of which there are also extensive remains.

*Continue on the D78E to Paradou and the D17 to the larger village of Maussane-les-Alpilles, leaving on the D78 east and passing the Rochers d'Entreconque. At the D24 turn left (view of La Caume). Pass the junction with the D25 and turn right on to the D24B to Eygalières.*

### Eygalières
The site of this attractive village was already old when the Romans built the aqueduct to Arles from here. Several medieval buildings remain, including the castle keep and the church, but more beautiful still is the view from the nearby Romanesque Chapelle St-Sixte (1.5km on the D24B).

*Turn left on to the D74A, crossing the Canal des Alpilles and joining the D99 for a scenic return to St-Rémy.*

**The Moulin de Daudet, which inspired Daudet's *Lettres de Mon Moulin***

# •ARLES•

42

**Capital of the Camargue, with a distinctive Provençal flavour, Arles is a small town on the Rhône with a lively Saturday market and a liking for bullfights. The Roman arena and theatre, together with the remarkable Romanesque cloister of St-Trophime and a rash of museums, are conveniently close in the centre of town and shouldn't be missed, but neither should a leisurely drink in the tiny place du Forum or a stroll through the market, for a taste of the town today.**

The survival of local folk tradition was ensured by Frédéric Mistral, poet and Nobel Prize-winner, born in nearby Maillane in 1830 and who was a member of the Félibrige Society, a group of Provençal poets writing in their native tongue. In 1904 Mistral used his prize money to buy the Hôtel Laval-Castellane and establish a museum of Provençal life. The Muséon Arlaten was the result – a fascinating collection of everything from porcelain to paintings, and from children's toys to reconstructed rooms.

Arles (map ref: 112 B2) is a major centre for festivals. Besides the main *Festival d'Arles* and international photography exhibition in July, *corridas* (bullfights) are a central part of local life but are not to everyone's taste. If you don't want to witness a *mise-à-mort* (to the death), look out for the Camargue-style *course à la cocarde*, where the *razeteurs* must remove ribbons or *cocardes* from the bull's horns before they

**The cathedral of St-Trophime, whose cloister is a fine example of Romanesque art**

can jump to safety outside the ring.

Arles is also capital of the Camargue's rice industry, and September is given over to celebrating *Les Prémices du Riz*, when a local Arlésienne is crowned *Ambassadrice du Riz* and competitions offer intriguing prizes of the winner's weight in rice.

The Rhône is a short walk from the centre of Arles. On the quai Marx Dormoy are the ruins of Constantine's palace, Roman baths and the Musée Réattu, a mixed collection including a series of drawings by Picasso, housed in the beautiful former priory of the Knights of Malta. Southeast of the centre, Les Alyscamps is a sadly depleted avenue of Roman and early Christian mausoleums and sarcophagi leading to the Church of St-Honorat, one of the sites which were painted by Vincent Van Gogh.

**Nearby** When the plains around Arles were marshes, the Abbaye de Montmajour was built on a rocky outcrop 6km to the northwest (N570, then D17). Saved from total ruin after its dissolution in the 18th century, the almost windowless abbey church and 14th-century defensive tower still make an impressive sight and a climb to the viewing platform is rewarded with panoramic views. On the ground, the high spot is the beautifully carved cloisters, with similarities to St-Trophime, and, beneath the church, a vaulted crypt.

**Back to nature** The Ecomusée which has been established at St-Martin-de-Crau, 16km west on the E80 or N113, is a good place to discover the native wildlife and traditional rural activities of Provence.

## FLAVOURS OF ARLES

Arles sausage, made from local *taureau* (bull meat), is on sale along with many other local specialities at the enormous market which lines the boulevard des Lices every Saturday, with a smaller version on Wednesdays. As well as food, look out for *brocante* (second-hand goods) and antiques around the Jardin d'Eté and traditional Provençal fabric towards the boulevard Georges Clemenceau. Several of Arles' more upmarket stores also sell this fabric, with its distinctive small design, along with the ubiquitous *santons* in traditional costume, which includes a lace coiffe similar to that worn by Breton women.

## TOWN WALK

If you plan to visit several of the historic sites, invest in a global ticket to save money. Different combinations available concentrate on the museums, the Roman monuments, or both.

*Start from the steps of the arena at the top of rue Voltaire.*

**1** Approaching from the north, the arches of the arena, which once held up to 20,000 spectators, loom ahead, crowded in by the surrounding buildings. Like the arena in Nîmes, it had to be cleared of houses and churches when it was restored in the 19th century. It can best be seen by climbing one of the three remaining towers added in the 12th century.

*Take the elevated Rond Point des Arènes past the Fondation Vincent Van Gogh in the Palais de Luppe to the Théâtre Antique, entrance in rue de la Calade.*

**2** After centuries of pillaging, there are fewer remains of the theatre, built in the reign of Augustus, but you get some idea of its former scale from the two pillars that form a magnificent backdrop for summer concerts.

*Turn left down rue du Cloître , then right for the cloister.*

**3** Together with the newly cleaned doorway of the cathedral next door, the Cloître St-Trophime is one of the most perfect pieces of Romanesque art in Provence, but can rarely be experienced as a tranquil haven at the height of summer. The cathedral has several treasures, including a beautiful statue of the Virgin by Leonardo

Murano (1619). Find the chapel of relics and look for the shoe of Jean-Marie Duclau, the martyred archbishop of Arles.

*Cross place de la République to the Musée Lapidaire d'Art Païen.*

**4** Pieces of Greek and Roman sarcophagi, mosaics and carvings, including casts of the Venus of Arles and a vast statue of Augustus, are displayed in the former Church of Ste-Anne.

*Walk through the Hôtel de Ville, bear left, then right to the place du Forum. The pillars set into the corner of the Nord-Pinus Hôtel come from a 2nd-century temple. Return to rue Balze and the Musée Lapidaire d'Art Chrétien.*

**5** As well as containing carved sarcophagi brought from the Alyscamps, the former Jesuit

### Espace Van Gogh

chapel with its monumental altar is also the entrance to the Cryptoporticus, the gallery that once ran beneath the forum.

*Turn left into rue Mistral and left again into the main shopping street, rue de la République, with the Muséon Arlaten on the left.*

**6** In rue du President-Wilson the Espace Van Gogh has been restored to its combination of bright blues and yellows.

*Turn left into the boulevard des Lices, past the tourist office, post office and Jardin d'Hiver, and cross the shady Jardin d'Eté, to return to the arena.*

**7** To the right of the arena across place de la Major, Notre-Dame is a blend of Romanesque and Gothic.

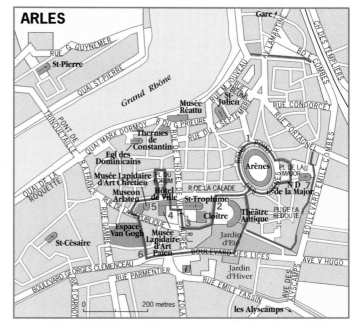

ARLES

# WRITERS, POETS AND ARTISTS

The vivid landscape, the climate and the relaxing ambience of Provence have acted like a magnet over the ages for writers, poets and, especially, painters. The first artist of note to be linked with the South – apart from Fragonard, who was born there but did most of his painting in Paris – was Cézanne.

Born into a wealthy family at Aix-en-Provence in 1839, Cézanne knew from childhood that he wanted to be a painter. His father sent him to art school in Paris, but he soon found that his very personal way of painting was not appreciated. If it hadn't been for the encouragement of his friend, the writer Emile Zola, Cézanne might well have given up. But when he was in his 40s, his father died, leaving him comfortably off. Cushioned by his inheritance, he became almost a recluse, setting up a studio near the town. Cézanne became obsessed by Montagne Ste-Victoire, which he featured in hundreds of pictures. Despite failing health, he continued to do paintings of the mountain right up to his death at the age of 67 in 1906. His studio on the outskirts of Aix is now a museum.

## ART IN THE SOUTH

'The future of modern art lies in the South of France' said Vincent Van Gogh prophetically when, having spent two years in Paris, he moved to Arles in 1888. He was at that time obsessed with the work of the Japanese artist Hokusai, and thought that by moving to the heat and colour of the South he would be in an atmosphere nearer to his fantasy image of Japan.

He set up a studio in the town which he planned to share with Gauguin, but the two men quarrelled a great deal, and one night Van Gogh threatened him with a razor. Gauguin hastily moved out, and in a rage Van Gogh cut off his own ear and gave it to a prostitute. He was taken to hospital, and then admitted himself to an asylum, the Maison de Santé at nearby St-Rémy-de-Provence.

It was at St-Rémy that Van Gogh painted some of his most famous works, notably *Irises, Cornfield with Cypresses* and *Starry Night*. Eventually he was discharged as 'cured' and went to stay near Paris under the care of a local doctor, who described his illness as 'Midi

Two works by artists who were captivated by the Provence magic: the Chapelle du Rosaire in Vence, designed by Matisse (above right); and *Peaches and Pears* by Cézanne

disease'. But he continued to suffer from depression and on 29 July 1890, at the age of 37, he shot himself.

Many of the places that Van Gogh immortalised on canvas have disappeared – the bridge at Arles, for instance, which was dismantled in 1926 and re-sited, and the original yellow café. But the asylum remains, and is now a psychiatric hospital named after him.

## DISCOVERY

The 'discovery' of St-Tropez has been credited to many people, but the first was probably the writer Guy de Maupassant, in 1888, who described it as a 'gay little city'. In 1892, the painter Paul Signac moved to the then unknown fishing village, triggering off an exodus south by fellow artists. A few years later, in 1907, the Impressionist Renoir bought a small estate along the coast near Cagnes-sur-Mer. In response to the brilliant Mediterranean light he produced a series of paintings, notably *The Bathers*, before his death in 1919.

The group of artists whose names will forever be linked with Provence, however, were the Fauves ('wild beasts') who, for a brief five years, painted vivid canvases of the South in bright vermilion, cobalt, viridian, and pinks. Names like Derain, Vlaminck and Marquet all descended upon the Mediterranean coast, together with Braque, who went on to become a cubist.

The leader of the group and greatest of them all, however, was Matisse, who made his home in Provence and the Riviera in particular. A lasting monument to his time there is the Chapelle du Rosaire at Vence, which he decorated in 1947. Born in 1869, Matisse spent most of his working life in and around Nice. In 1938 he settled on the outskirts of Cimiez, where he died in November 1954.

Many other painters have been associated with Provence: Chagall lived for a time at Gordes, before settling finally at Vence. Max Ernst also lived in the Midi, making his home there for a while. But the most famous of the postwar group is, of course, Picasso, who came to Provence in 1945, it is said, because it reminded him of his native Spain.

He stayed first at a château in Antibes, then moved inland to Vallauris where he began making his famous pottery. Finally he established himself in a large house which has been kept by his family near the village of Vauvenargues on the slopes of Montagne Ste-Victoire. In his last years Picasso moved to the more accessible coastal village of Mougins, where he died, aged 90, in 1973.

Of the artists who are linked with Provence today, one of the best known is Vasarély, who has restored the château in the centre of Gordes to house a permanent exhibition of his abstract art. Near by, another abstract painter, Brigid Riley, has a house near St-Saturnin-d'Apt, where she works for several months of the year.

## POETRY

Provence has had a history of poetry since the days of the 12th and 13th centuries when troubadours went from court to court singing their verses of love. Then came Petrarch (1304–74) who was brought up in Carpentras, and then went to Avignon to study. It was here that he caught a glimpse of the beautiful Laura, and embarked on a one-sided love affair. Laura haunted him long after her death in 1348, and he immortalised her in his now famous sonnets.

Provençal literature was reborn in the 19th century when a group of seven young poets, the best-known of whom was Mistral, met together in Arles in 1854 to form a society called the Félibrige. Their aim was to revive and write in the old Provençal language. Mistral went on to publish an epic poem which Gounod made into an opera, and in 1904 he was awarded the Nobel Prize for literature. Alphonse Daudet, author of *Lettres de Mon Moulin*, was also linked with the Félibrige society, as was Emile Zola.

## LITERATURE

The warm South has also played host to such notable French writers as Jean Giono, Marcel Pagnol, and René Char. Writers from abroad, too, have always been attracted to the South of France. The list is endless: Friedrich Nietzsche, Frank Harris, Robert Louis Stevenson. Scott Fitzgerald lived for a while on the Riviera, while Colette made St-Tropez her home in the 1930s. During the last war, Samuel Becket is believed to have thought up his famous play *Waiting for Godot,* while standing at a crossroads near Roussillon – where he lived for a while in 1942. More recently Lawrence Durrell spent his last years in a country farm near Nîmes, and wrote a book about his long love affair with Provence.

The memorial to Vincent Van Gogh in Arles

## AUBAGNE

MAP REF: 112 C2

Once ringed by walls, this small market town is now surrounded on all sides by *autoroutes* and has been all but swallowed up by the suburbs east of Marseille. Marcel Pagnol was born here in 1895 and re-created the memories of his early years in the area in word and film – *Jean de Florette* and *Manon des Sources*. Ask at the Syndicat d'Initiative for details if you want to visit Pagnol sites, including the village where he spent childhood holidays and later shot some of his films.

For 30 years Aubagne has been the home of the French Foreign Legion, the Légion Etrangère, whose headquarters to the west of town include the Musée du Képi Blanc, commemorating the legion's service in Algeria (restricted opening out of season). **For children** For a break from sightseeing, OK Corral lies 16km east on the N8 – a large and popular amusement park with rides that should satisfy even the bravest appetite for adventure. **Nearby** Motor-racing enthusiasts should cross the D2 and continue on the N8 to the Autodrome, better known as the Circuit Paul Ricard and once scene of the annual French Grand Prix, while 5km northeast of Aubagne, at the start of the picturesque winding route through the Massif de la Ste-Baume, Gemenos boasts a late 17th-century château.

## BARBENTANE

MAP REF: 112 B3

Near the confluence of the Durance and the Rhône, on the slopes of a series of hills known as La Montagnette, Barbentane's 17th-century château reveals superb ornate interiors behind its simple classical façade. The past strategic importance of the village is apparent from the remains of its medieval fortifications – including the Tour Angelica, part of a previous castle – and the crumbling Renaissance Maison des Chevaliers, near the Church of Notre-Dame-de-Grâce.
**Nearby** South in the hills of La Montagnette, Boulbon is another village more important in the past than today. The remains of its walls and mighty fortress are still evident, and outside the village are two well-preserved chapels dedicated to St-Marcellin and St-Julien.

A visit to the Abbaye de St-Michel-de-Frigolet, where poet Frédéric Mistral (see page 45) was once a pupil, includes the 12th-century church and cloister and the fantastically colourful 19th-century addition, as well as a chance to buy some of the abbey's own liqueur, distilled from local herbs.

## BAUX-DE-PROVENCE, LES

MAP REF: 112 B2

Even in the searing heat of summer, few visitors to this, one of Provence's most famous sights, would choose to miss it. Clinging to an outcrop of the Alpilles, the Renaissance town of Les Baux is today almost totally dependent on tourism. After its destruction by Richelieu in the 17th century, it did not revive until the discovery, 200 years later, of the aluminium-bearing mineral, bauxite, named after the village.

Complementing the beautiful Renaissance mansions of the lower village is the upper Cité Morte, which you must pay to enter. Here you will find the medieval castle where 13th-century troubadours sang and 14th-century Raymond de Turenne forced his prisoners to jump to their death from the walls of the keep, now standing ruined and abandoned. The views alone from the Tour Parvelle over the village, and the sweeping

**Camargue wildlife: a crane and flamingos share a lagoon**

panorama from the southern tip of the rock, make the entrance fee worthwhile. In the lower village, look out for the Hôtel de Manville, now the Hôtel de Ville, and Romanesque St-Vincent Church with its Renaissance *lanterne des morts*.
**Nearby** Many of the strange rock formations in the Val d'Enfer (Valley of Hell), a short way northwest of the village on the D27, pre-date the 19th-century bauxite mining, but some of the largest quarries have been transformed into the Cathédrale d'Images, a giant sound and light show projected on to every available surface.

## CAMARGUE

MAP REF: 112 A2/B2

In 1970 the marshy delta between the two arms of the Rhône was designated the Parc Naturel Régional de Camargue, a unique landscape of saltmarshes (*sansouires*) and lagoons dotted with black bulls, pink flamingos and the white horses of the *gardian* cowboys. Tourism is an increasingly important element in that landscape, not only in the main town of Stes-Maries-de-la-Mer (see page 57), but for the *mas* or farms of the Camargue, as the practice of bull-rearing becomes less profitable and the interest of visitors more so.

**Prisoners once jumped from the walls of the keep in the Cité Morte, Les Baux-de-Provence; now tourists climb the ruins for good views**

Several museums illustrate different facets of the landscape: the excellent Musée Camarguais, at the Mas du Pont de Rousty off the D570, is the best introduction to its history and has a 3.5km marked trail; at Le Sambuc, on the D36, the Musée du Riz de Camargue describes the production of France's biggest rice crop on former salt pans that were irrigated with fresh water; and on the D570, the elegant Château d'Avignon has a rich collection of 19th-century furnishing.

Access to the main Etang de Vaccarès itself is limited. A series of paths and dikes allow you to see some of the many species of plants, birds and animals, but for a guaranteed sighting, visit the Parc Ornithologique du Pont-de-Gau, where large aviaries show the rarer species, and the nearby park information centre at Ginès. You can explore the Camargue from the water aboard a restored paddle-steamer, the *Tiki III* which departs from the mouth of the Petit-Rhône and heads upstream (follow the D38 to Aigues-Mortes), or in traditional *gardian* style on horseback – the Syndicat d'Initiative has a list of nearby stables offering guided rides.

## CYCLE TOUR

Cycling is a good way to explore the flat, sometimes blustery distances of the Camargue. The *Digue à la Mer*, or sea dike, between the long beach and the Etang de Vaccarès, is exclusively for walkers and cyclists. You will need to retrace your steps if you plan to visit the lighthouse, Phare de la Gacholle, a bracing 12km from Stes-Maries, or the flamingo nesting site at Etang du Fangassier, although motorists have an easier approach from the Salin-de-Giraud end.

This circular route is only 20km and makes an excellent cycle tour. There are several rental places in Stes-Maries (if in doubt, the Syndicat d'Iniative near the beach has a list).

Leave Stes-Maries on the D85A, which runs between the Réserve Départementale des Impériaux et du Malagroy on your right and the Etang de Ginès on the left. After 4km, from where there's a good view east near the Mas de Cacharel, the road bears left, while an alternative route branches off right to Méjanes.

After 6km the D85 joins the D570 at Pioch-Badet: for a longer trip, turn right and cycle 5km to the Château d'Avignon. Heading south back towards Stes-Maries will

bring you past the Centre d'Information de Ginès and the Parc Ornithologique du Pont-de-Gau. To return along the banks of the Petit-Rhône, turn right on to the D85 just before the Musée de Cire (wax museum) and left on to the D38, which loops back into Stes-Maries around the Etang des Launes.

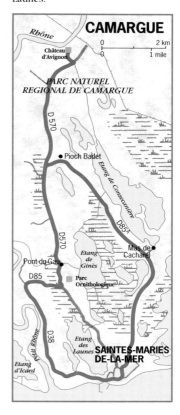

## CARRY-LE-ROUET

### MAP REF: 112 C2

West of Marseille and backed by the limestone hills of the Chaîne de l'Estaque, a series of old fishing villages and nearby beaches have grown into small resorts, which are particularly popular with locals trying to avoid the crush and crowds at the better-known resorts further east. The largest and most popular of these, Carry-le-Rouet, clusters around its small port with holiday villas set among the surrounding pines. To the east of Carry-le-Rouet there are good views over le Rouet Plage, as the road climbs through the Vallon de l'Aigle (Eagle's Valley). A couple of kilometres along the coast to the west of the resort are the smaller villages of Sausset-les-Pins and Carro.

## CASSIS

### MAP REF: 112 C1

This fashionable small port, known for its fish restaurants and crisp white wine, may soon be equally famous for a series of multi-coloured cave paintings recently discovered along the coast and thought to be over 10,000 years old (the paintings have yet to be authenticated). In the meantime Cassis is the best place to take a boat trip to the most famous of the *calanques*, or inlets, that cut into the limestone cliffs along the coast on both sides of Marseille. Boats depart from the

**Boats in line at Cassis**

quai St-Pierre for the deep turquoise waters of Port-Miou, Port-Pin and En-Vau, each *calanque* prettier than the last. You can also reach the secluded beaches at the head of the creeks on foot, by following the GR98b footpath from beyond the plage du Bestouan.

The setting of Cassis itself is superb, and in the height of the summer it is inevitably crowded. The lure of seafood and fish restaurants may mean that you don't want to stroll further than the quays, but off place Baragnon and near the modern casino, the municipal museum (afternoons

**Stylish seafood restaurants line the pretty quays of Cassis, a popular little port with access to the inlets around Marseille**

only) on rue Xavier-d'Authier gives a good insight into other aspects of Cassis, while the promenade des Lombards heads out south towards the Pointe des Lombards, past the restored 12th-century fortress of the lords of Les Baux (now a private residence).
**Nearby** The D141 is a spectacular coast road southeast to La Ciotat, climbing past precipitous views from the Cap Canaille and the Grande Tête.

## CIOTAT, LA

*MAP REF: 112 C1*

Halfway between Marseille and Toulon, La Ciotat has long been primarily a shipbuilding town, which, like its giant neighbours, has suffered from relying on an industry in recession. The quayside of the *vieux port*, however, has all the charm of many old ports. Behind the waterfront, buildings of interest are mainly ecclesiastic – in particular the handsome 17th-century Notre-Dame de l'Assomption overlooking the port, as well as the Chapels of the Blue and Black Penitents. But for a different perspective on the town, and the eagle-shaped Cap d'Aigle, make the short boat trip to the small offshore island, the Ile Verte.

North of the old town, the resort of La Ciotat-Plage offers the more traditional coastal combination of beaches and expensive hotels, while film enthusiasts should note the statue commemorating the

**The two faces of La Ciotat: boats crowding into the harbour and, as a backdrop, ecclesiastical buildings lining the waterfront**

Lumière brothers' first showing of their motion pictures here in 1895.

**Nearby** A short distance west, the coast is indented with more *calanques*, including the Calanque de Figuerolles, which is easily reached from the avenue des Calanques.

## FOS

*MAP REF: 112 B2*

Should you want to take a closer look at the modern monuments of oil refineries and tanker terminals that make up the vast Fos industrial complex, you can join a guided boat tour or visit the information centre at La Fosette, 8km inland on the N568. Squeezed between the oil tanks and the Etang de l'Estomac is Fos-sur-Mer, a small town already in existence at the time of Roman Gaul. With its Romanesque church and substantial remains of a medieval castle and walls, it is a good place to see the strange juxtaposition of old and new that is so characteristic of the area around the Etang de Berre. The 18th-century harbour of Port-St-Louis-du-Rhône, at the mouth of the

Grand Rhône is now a giant roll-on-roll-off port, although St-Mitre-les-Remparts, on the lagoon itself, has maintained its peace along with its medieval fortified walls.

**For history buffs** At St-Blaise, archaeological excavations around a small Romanesque chapel show that signs of settlement here stretch back to at least the 6th century BC, with some impressive Greek ramparts later incorporated into an early medieval settlement. A museum displays pottery and other finds from the dig.

The D10 crosses the River Touloubre southeast of St-Chamas in particularly grand style via the Pont Flavien, a single-span Roman bridge with a triumphal arch at each end.

**Nearby** Following the western shore of the lagoon north, the landscape is less industrialised, more scenic. Istres is a modern town with Greek roots and a good museum of local history and geography, including archaeological remains retrieved from the seabed of the Golfe de Fos. The villages of Miramas-le-Vieux, perched on its rocky hilltop, and Cornillon-Confoux are particularly pretty.

# FOOD AND DRINK

The food of Provence gives you an instant taste of sunshine. Never subtle – the strong flavours of olive oil, anchovies and garlic tend to predominate – it is substantial and colourful. Even its greatest devotees would not describe Provençal cuisine as among the most elegant in France, yet strangely enough, the most famous chef in the world, Escoffier, was born here in 1846, at Villeneuve-Loubet, between Nice and Cannes.

**Beauty from commerce: herb fields in Provence**

## A TASTE OF THE SOUTH

Provençal cuisine has a magical character that echoes the Mediterranean. Dairy produce disappears off the menu here in the South, and the olive tree takes over. Provençal olive oil is particularly strongly flavoured compared with that of, say, Italy, and dominates most meals. Whether it is used to make *aïoli*, the famous garlic-flavoured mayonnaise or to provide an under-taste in a *daube*, or a *tian*, the taste is always there.

Herbs figure strongly too – every Provençal housewife has her pot of basil growing on the windowsill in summer for dishes like *soupe au pistou*, a traditional vegetable soup flavoured with a paste made from basil, olive oil and pine nuts. Thyme and oregano are used in abundance too, as is pungent anise-flavoured fennel.

## MORE THAN A SOUP

Proximity to the Mediterranean means that much of the best food features fish. Provence's most famous dish is probably the saffron-coloured *bouillabaisse*. More than just a soup, it is a meal in itself, a melange of innumerable sorts of fish including conger eel, spider crabs and a small ugly-looking red fish, the *rascasse*, that is its most important ingredient. The faint-hearted, who don't want to grapple with fish heads and tails, should order the more elegant *soupe de poisson*, in which the fish is sieved.

Both of these classic soups are accompanied by grated cheese and *aïoli*, or more usually *rouille*, a spicy, more peppery sauce. *Bourride* is another more elegant fish dish. Here only white fish is used, poached in a white stock and served with a sauce made with *aïoli*. As with *bouillabaisse*, it is served in two stages – first of all as a soup and then as the main dish.

## A TASTE OF ITALY

*Pissaladière,* a speciality of Nice, is a tart made from yeast dough, anchovies, olives and tomatoes flavoured with basil, which looks and tastes very much like a pizza. You'll also find *aigo-boulido,* a cousin of the classic Italian minestrone soup. With so many sun-loving vegetables to draw on, it's not surprising that aubergines and peppers feature in many dishes, notably *ratatouille,* a mix of vegetables simmered in olive oil, and the famous *salade Niçoise,* where peppers are combined with crisp lettuce, hard-boiled eggs, olives and, frequently, tuna.

## TRADITIONAL DISHES

Away from the tourist area you will encounter all kinds of peasant dishes – *pieds et paquets,* for instance (sheep's tripe folded into neat little parcels and cooked with trotters, tomatoes and wine), and *tians,* named after the shallow dish in which they are cooked, usually a baked mix of vegetables with egg. Another dish, which is an acquired taste, is *brandade de morue,* salt cod that has been soaked, then pounded into a paste with cream and olive oil then served with toasted chunks of French bread. The *daube* is another famous Provençal country dish, a hearty beef casserole traditionally cooked overnight on the fire in a sealed pot called a *daubière.* A *daube* should traditionally have a pig's trotter in it to give it that slightly gelatinous consistency. A Provençal meal often starts with *tapenade,* a paste made from capers and anchovies pounded with olive oil and lemon, or *anchoïade,* with a stronger flavour of anchovies, blended with oil and vinegar.

Provence is truffle country, and the fungi that have been called black gold fetch astronomical prices in the markets. This is reflected in restaurants too, where a simple truffle omelette may be one of the most expensive items on the menu.

## NORTH AFRICAN INFLUENCE

With Marseille being the nearest French port to Algiers, the North African influence makes itself felt in Provençal cuisine with *cous-cous,* a dish that usually consists of a mix of chicken and lamb with seven vegetables, including chick peas. It is accompanied by the *cous-cous* itself, ground semolina rolled into minute grains and served like rice, together with a fiery red sauce called *harissa,* which is made from pounded hot chillies and other spices.

Stocking up on French bread...

## DAIRY PRODUCE

Provençal cheeses are made from sheep's or goats' milk, rather than cows' milk. There are two types of goat cheese: the creamy fresh variety, such as the famous Banon cheese; and others that have been aged and pack a pungent smell and a salty taste. These usually come wrapped in chestnut leaves.

## WINES AND SPIRITS

Provençal wine matches the food in its strength. The best wines come from the Côtes du Rhône area north of Avignon, where Châteauneuf-du-Pape reigns supreme. There are many other powerful reds to try – Vacqueras, for instance, and Gigondas – but be warned: they are usually 13 per cent proof. Rosés, ideal for drinking chilled on hot summer nights, vary in quality and seldom travel well out of the country. However, Bandol and Tavel have acquired an international reputation and are the best names to look for on the wine list.

The wine producers of Provence are making a determined effort to improve the quality of their wines. Many new names are coming into vogue, notably in the Lubéron, where Château Isolette and Château la Canorgue can hold their own with many other classic French wines. White wines are harder to come by, as the climate is too hot to suit the right grapes, but the best ones to look for are those originating from Palette, near Aix-en-Provence, and the area around Cassis.

The traditional drink in Provence is *pastis,* an anise-flavoured spirit that turns milky-white when you add water. The most popular brand of all was invented by Paul Ricard. The traditional flavourings for this drink are fennel, mint and liquorice, but M Ricard, son of a wine-merchant, added some extra ingredients all his own and with great flair promoted his drink, particularly in the 1950s, so that it became a best seller.

...and wine: Châteauneuf-du-Pape

Domaine Pierre USSÉGLIC
*Propriétaire* *Récoltant*

Châteauneuf du Pape

ENTE EN BOUTEILLES · EXPÉDITIO
VERKAUF VON FLASCHEN

# •MARSEILLE•

Whatever you expect from Marseille, it shouldn't be Côte d'Azur glamour: France's second largest city literally turns its back on the resorts further east, too busy getting a living from the sea for their indulgent sun-basking. This is a working city, where the latest scandal of the finance-stricken Olympique Marseille football team is the topic of the day, and where the port of la Joliette has long been the arrival point for migrant workers and refugees – whether from Greece, Italy, Armenia or most recently Algeria – a potentially explosive ingredient in a city with a reputation for racism.

**A view of modern Marseille: toll-booths bringing the traffic to a brief halt on an autoroute leading into the city**

Marseille (map ref: 112 C2) is a monumental, rather than beautiful place, certainly vital, with some excellent museums – and of course, the best *bouillabaisse* anywhere. There is corruption, violence and drug abuse here as there is in any big city, and Marseille seems to suffer more than most. Though much of the crime is gang-based, don't invite trouble with a dangling handbag or unguarded camera.

Getting your bearings in the city centre is fairly straightforward, thanks to the famous main thoroughfare of La Canabière, which runs east-west to the rectangular *vieux port*. Standing on the quai des Belges, looking out to sea and the forts of St-Jean and St-Nicolas, the quarter to your left has a grid street plan, with some of the best restaurants in the pedestrianised area around the cours Jean Ballard. The jumble of streets climbing up to your right is the Le Panier quarter, the oldest part of the city and almost totally destroyed during World War II. Here, and north of La Canabière, are the most accessible remains of 6th-century BC Greek *Massalia* and Roman *Massilia*. And wherever you are in the city, you can always see the enormous neo-Byzantine church of Notre-Dame-de-la-Garde, topped by a 3m statue of the Virgin. It's worth the drive up to see the city nestling in its basin of limestone hills, its streets spread out below.

While there is a concentration around the port of museums depicting Marseille's history and development, there are several other museums and monuments worth seeking out on a visit to the city.

South of La Canabière, on rue de Grignan, the Musée Cantini has an excellent collection of modern

and contemporary painting and sculpture, together with a gallery of much older Moustiers porcelain.

Continuing east from La Canabière, the boulevard Longchamp leads to the elaborate Palais Longchamp, whose curved colonnade and central fountain join the Musée des Beaux Arts (on the left) and the Musée d'Histoire Naturelle. Opposite, at the end of the boulevard itself, the 19th-century mansion that was home to the rich bourgeois Grobet-Labardié family is now a perfect shrine to the taste and achievements of their age, furnished with their collection of fine tapestries, paintings and old musical instruments.

Southwest of the *vieux port*, the basilica of St-Victor is very different from the 19th-century confection of Notre-Dame-de-la-Garde above it. Dating from the 5th century, when it was built over the tombs of 3rd-century martyrs, the church was later rebuilt and fortified, although the crypt is original and was indeed found to contain early Christian sarcophagi.

Beyond Fort St-Nicolas at the entrance to the port, the gardens of Napoleon III's Château du Pharo make an excellent vantage point for views back over the city. **Nearby** The Corniche Président Kennedy follows the coast around from the Parc du Pharo towards the Parc Borély, whose château previously held the archaeological collection now in the Musée de la Vieille-Charité.

The avenue du Prado and boulevard du Michelet lead south to Le Corbusier's once celebrated *Cité Radieuse*, a series of blocks raised on stilts built according to the architect's theory of the *unité d'habitation*, but now rather less than radical.

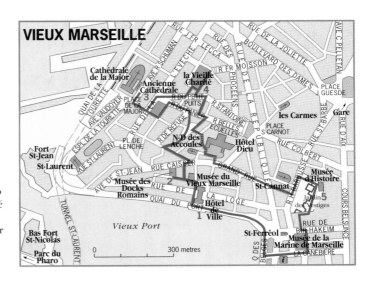

VIEUX MARSEILLE

## THE CHATEAU D'IF

A trip to the island fortress of the Château d'If is as memorable for the boat ride (regular departures from the quai des Belges) and the views from the island as for the grim former prison itself. Though the fortress is perhaps most notorious for the imprisonment of a fictitious prisoner – Alexandre Dumas' Count of Monte-Cristo – many real prisoners suffered here too, including Aix's Mirabeau and countless Huguenots during the times of religious persecution.

## TOWN WALK

*Starting from the quai des Belges (scene of the morning fish market), follow the quai du Port along the right side of the water to the Hôtel de Ville.*

1 This handsome baroque building was one of the few to be spared during the Nazi destruction of Le Panier's maze of streets in 1943.

*Turn right, away from the port, cross place Jules Verne and turn left for place Vivaux.*

2 Marseille's maritime history is explained at the Musée des Docks Romains with exhibits from Roman quayside warehouses, discovered here during postwar excavations of Le Panier. Returning to place Jules Verne, the beautiful 16th-century Maison Diamantée, named for its Italianate studded façade, houses the Musée du Vieux Marseille, an interesting collection of local furniture, costume, folk art and *santons*.

*Pass place du Mazeau, turn left and climb the Montée des Accoules (passing the Gothic bell-tower from the Notre-Dame des Accoules). Turn right into la ruelle des Moulins, through the place and rue des Muettes, left into rue de Panier and left again into rue Baussengue; pass the former Archbishop's Palace to reach the two cathedrals.*

3 The huge domed and striped neo-Byzantine Cathedral de la Major completely dominates its Romanesque predecessor, the Ancienne Cathédrale, which sits in its southern shadow.

*Return to rue de l'Evêche,*

*continuing as far as rue du Petits Puits to the right.*

4 The elegant restored building with arcaded galleries surrounding a domed chapel is la Vieille Charité, a cultural centre and the city's archaeological museum, designed in the 17th century as an almshouse by Pierre Puget.

*Head south again, turning left at rue du Panier, and then dropping down past the Hôtel-Dieu and Chapelle des Pénitents-Blancs. Turn left into Grand Rue, passing the Hôtel de Cabre and cross the main rue de la République.*

5 Behind the Bourse shopping centre, and discovered during its excavation, the Jardin des Vestiges is a small attractive garden where you can sit among the ruins of Greek *Massalia*. Inside the shopping centre is the entrance to the Musée d'Histoire de Marseille, whose star exhibit is the preserved hull of a Roman boat. On the ground floor of the Bourse itself is the Musée de la Marine and opposite, on place Général-de-Gaulle, is a statue of Pierre Puget.

## MARTIGUES

*MAP REF: 112 B2*

There have been settlements around the Etang de Berre since at least Roman times. The vast, shallow lagoon is separated from the Golfe de Fos by a range of limestone hills, the Chaîne de L'Estaque, breached at their western end by the Canal de Caronte, and the town of Martigues (another derivation from 'Dead Water', see page 40) guards the entry of the canal into the lagoon.

Though the suburbs have sprawled unattractively, the 16th-century heart of the town has been contained on the Ile Brescon. The 17th-century church of Ste-Madeleine de l'Ile and the view of colourful shuttered houses along the quays from the Pont St-Sébastien (known as the *Miroir aux Oiseaux*) attracted many artists, and the works of one, Félix Ziem, are commemorated in the Musée Ziem in the Ferrières quarter north of the island.

(For other towns on the Etang de Berre, see Fos, page 49.)

## MASSIF DE LA STE-BAUME

*MAP REF: 112 C2*

The legend of the three Marys' arrival in Provence (see Stes-Maries-de-la-Mer, page 57) continues with Mary Magdalen's retreat in penance to a cave high in this vast, partly forested *massif*, making it an important shrine and pilgrimage site ever since. **Nearby** Twenty kilometres north of the *grotte* (D80, then N560) the small town of St-Maximin-la-Ste-Baume clusters around the Gothic basilica of Ste-Madeleine, built over tombs discovered in the 12th century and said to be those of Mary Magdalen and St-Maximus, who had accompanied the two Marys from the Holy Land. In contrast to the simplicity of the *grotte*, the church has a profusion of art treasures, including a magnificent 16th-century retable, which is to the left behind the high altar.

## COUNTRY WALK

The route to the *grotte* ends in a long flight of steps, with the option of continuing up to the monument at the summit of the peak, St-Pilon (994m).

*The path, which is part of the long-distance GR9 footpath, leaves the D80 to the left of the cemetery, next to the Hôtellerie de la Ste-Baume.*

Climb upwards through the high cover of beech trees – unusual for a Provençal forest, but explained by the cold micro-climate of the northern lee of the mountains – for 1.5km until you reach a crossroads marked by an oratory (the Carrefour de l'Oratoire).

*Bear right and climb the flight of 150 steps past the calvary to the pietà beneath the cave itself, with a statue of the saint and an altar where Mass is celebrated annually.*

To reach the summit of St-Pilon, return to the Carrefour de l'Oratoire and turn right, climbing past the Chapelle des Parisiens and another oratory and bearing right at the Col du St-Pilon. The view from the top more than rewards the climb.

*For a circular return from the Carrefour de l'Oratoire, take the path to the left of the fountain, passing a large oratory on the right after about 1km. If you don't want to return to the Hôtellerie along the D80, take the footpath to the left just before the road.*

## NIMES

*MAP REF: 112 A3*

Though not strictly in Provence, as it lies across the Rhône in Languedoc-Roussillon, Nîmes not only shares a common Roman heritage with the cities of the Bouches-du-Rhône, but also has a distinctly Provençal cuisine. Like nearby Montpellier, Nîmes has recently embarked on an ambitious programme of development, with world-class architects employed to create modern monuments such as the Médiathèque, opposite the Roman Maison Carré (a 1st-century AD temple), the Abribus Stark (rue Notre-Dame) and some delightful new fountains.

Despite its awesome Roman legacy, the town which gave the world denim (*serge de Nîmes*) has been influenced more by its prosperity from the Protestant-dominated textile industry than by any cultural aspirations. **For children** Children weary of ancient cultures might like to investigate the Videothèque in the new Carrée d'Art or visit the Planétarium, next to the Mont Duplan amusement park in the northwest of town.

## PONT DU GARD

*MAP REF: 112 B3*

The solitary splendour of the Pont du Gard is one of the most familiar images of the Roman legacy, but the encroaching commercialism on the banks of the Gardon might come as something of a shock. Built in 19BC as part of a 50km aqueduct to supply water to Nîmes, the bridge is remarkable, and those with a head for heights can cross on foot.

54

**Facing page: the Maison Carrée at Nîmes**
**Right: the Pont du Gard**

**Nearby** Equally well-preserved is the small town of Uzès, northwest of the Pont du Gard (22km north of Nîmes) in the heart of the limestone *garrigue* country. The narrow streets and arcaded squares that cluster around the mighty ducal palace are lined with grand Renaissance *hôtels* dating from its years of prosperity as a linen and silk centre, and the six-storey Tour Fenestrelle next to St-Théodorat Cathedral is unique.

## TOWN WALK

Any exploration of Nîmes should include a visit to the beautiful Jardin de la Fontaine, refashioned in the elegant style of the 18th century on the site of Roman temples and baths around the original spring of Nemausus.

*Start in place du Marché.*

1 The delightful modern bronze fountain of a crocodile, part of the city's crest, was originally granted by the Emperor Augustus; it represented the defeat of Mark Antony in Egypt, hence the chain attached to the palm tree.

*Take rue Fresque south to the Roman arena.*

2 In an even better state of repair than that of Arles, the 5th-century *Arènes*, measuring 132m by 105m, has recently acquired an adjustable roof so that it can be used as a theatre all year round.

*Rue de l'Aspic has some of Nîmes' finest mansions. Turn right into rue Pelliet and bear left to rue des Marchands (see the Passage des Marchands), which leads to the place aux Herbes.*

3 The former Bishop's Palace, to the right, now houses the Musée du Vieux Nîmes, and while the cathedral of St-Castor might at first appear Romanesque from its façade, it was rebuilt in the 19th century.

*Rue des Halles leads to the large covered market on rue Général Perrier. Turn left and continue to the Maison Carrée.*

4 It is easy to forget that this perfectly proportioned temple is over 2,000 years old. It houses a museum today, but like the arena has been treated with less dignity in the past, even being used as a stable in the 16th century.

*Turn right into rue Auguste (the tourist office is on the right) and left at square Antonin, following the elegant quai de la Fontaine along the canal.*

5 The Jardin de la Fontaine is Nîmes' most overlooked corner. The sacred spring itself is now neatly channelled between 18th-century balustrades. Visit the Castellum northeast of square Antonin, via rue du Fort.

*Return to the Maison Carrée via the place d'Assas. Rue de l'Horloge, south of the temple, leads back to the heart of old Nîmes. Turn right into rue de l'Aspic, then right and left to rue de Bernis and rue Fresque, returning to place du Marché.*

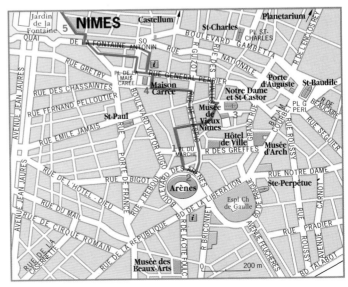

## ST-REMY-DE-PROVENCE

*MAP REF: 112 B3*

This small town, 25km northeast of Arles across the Chaîne des Alpilles, makes a perfect base for exploring the region (see drive on page 41). It has everything a Provençal town should have – from works by Van Gogh to a lively market (on Wednesdays and Saturdays) – within a compact, historic core ringed by plane-tree-lined boulevards.

Between St-Rémy and the Alpilles stands remarkable evidence of the area's long history: two Roman monuments known as *Les Antiques,* and *Glanum,* a ruined Roman settlement of which there is still much to see and which makes a pleasant walk from the town centre.

Some of the oldest houses in the town itself can be seen in rue Hoche, one of the most dilapidated being the birthplace, in 1503, of Michel de Nostredame, who was to earn lasting fame first as a royal physician and then for his astrological predictions. An elegant fountain commemorates him on rue Carnot.

The town's most attractive square is the shady place Favier, where the restored Hôtel de Mistral Mondragon is connected by a stone arch to the Hôtel de Sade, both housing excellent museums. The first is the Musée des Alpilles, with exhibitions explaining the geology and ecology of the Alpilles, local history and tradition. But the house itself, with its interior courtyard, is perhaps most interesting of all. The Hôtel de Sade houses the archaeological museum, with many of the finds from *Glanum*, together with relics of prehistoric life in the area. Investing in a global ticket for *Glanum* and the two museums will save you money if you intend to visit all three.

Place de la République, the main square, is overlooked by the giant pillars of the church of St-Martin. Beyond the 19th-century façade, rebuilt after an earlier church collapsed leaving only the bell tower, the interior reveals some interesting murals and bas-reliefs, but the most dramatic feature by far is the organ above the doorway – a marvellous green and orange confection installed in 1983 as the latest in a long line of organs stretching back to the 12th century.

The most recent and attractive restoration has been the transformation of the Hôtel Estrine, 8 rue Estrine, into the Centre d'Art Présence Van Gogh. The beautiful mansion was originally built in the 18th century; today the simple white stone arches are complemented by a black wrought-iron balustrade. As well as the permanent exhibition on the life and works of Van Gogh, the centre stages major exhibitions, and you can buy a reproduction of your favourite from the well-stocked shop (closed Mondays).

The walk or drive to St-Paul-de-Mausole and *Glanum,* south of the town, passes several other places of interest. Avenue Maillane meets avenue Pasteur at the Chapelle Notre-Dame de Pitié which houses the paintings of the Donation Mario Prassinos. The remarkable arch and mausoleum, *Les Antiques,* which stand to the side of the avenue Vincent Van Gogh, show the prosperity of the Gallo-Roman town, which was eventually sacked and abandoned in the third century. The extensive remains of *Glanum* itself stand opposite and include houses, temples, baths, the forum, the Nymphean spring and mosaics. Returning towards St-Rémy, the allées St-Paul lead to the Romanesque church and cloister of St-Paul. Van Gogh painted many of the nearby landmarks, including the Mas St-Paul, the Champ de Coquelicots gardens and La Carrière, a series of troglodyte dwellings, now an agricultural museum.

**The legendary Camargue bulls, guarded by mounted herdsmen, are used in bullfights**

MARKET WED.

## SALON-DE-PROVENCE
### MAP REF: 112 B2

After seeing the birthplace of Nostradamus in St-Rémy, you can visit the house where he spent his final and most prolific years in Salon-de-Provence, a large agricultural town 30km west of Aix-en-Provence on the Autoroute du Soleil. The Maison de Nostradamus, now a museum dedicated to the life of the astrologer, stands in the heart of the old town, near the 13th-century church of St-Michel and the elegant Hôtel-de-Ville. The church where he is buried, the 14th-century St-Laurent, lies further north via rue des Frères-Kennedy or rue Maréchal Joffre.

In addition to the reputation of its most famous adopted son, the town is dominated physically by the Château de l'Empéri, dating from the 10th century and housing a museum of the French army.

**Nearby** For its first 7km, the N538 north from Salon follows the Canal de Craponne, named after the local engineer, Adam de Craponne, who constructed the waterway between the Durance and the Etang de Berre in the 16th century. The best local viewpoint is from the ruins of Vieux Vernègues, 12km northeast of Salon via the D16 or D68 to Vernègues and then uphill to the abandoned hilltop village.

Tarascon's Renaissance castle, towering over the waters of the River Rhône

## STES-MARIES-DE-LA-MER
### MAP REF: 112 A2

MARKET MON FRI

This gaudy village, where *gardians* ride through the streets for the tourists, is the unattractive face of the Camargue (see page 46). It is named for the three Marys – Mary Magdalen, Mary Salomé (the mother of James and John the Apostles), and Mary (the sister or sister-in-law of the Virgin) – who were said to have landed here by boat from the Holy Land with their servant Sarah (see Tarascon and the Massif de la Ste-Baume). But it is Sarah, the patron saint of gypsies, who is the main focus of the famous annual festival. The black statue of Sarah, often draped in chiffon, can be seen in the crypt of the fortified Romanesque church, on to whose roof you can climb for views of the coast and the Camargue.

Across place Lamartine from the church, the Musée Baroncelli illustrates the traditional life and customs of the Camargue.

A sandy beach stretches east from the village, backed by a dike (*digue*) which you can explore on foot or by bicycle. Ask at the tourist office on avenue Van Gogh for a list of addresses for bicycle rental; for other suggested rides, see page 47.

## THE FESTIVAL

Gypsies from all over Europe make the pilgrimage to Stes-Maries for the festival of Ste-Sarah on 24 and 25 May, when first the statue of the saint and then effigies of the two Marys are carried into the sea, to be blessed along with the Camargue and its people. There is another, smaller celebration in late October.

## TARASCON
### MAP REF: 112 B3

MARKET TUES

It is sometimes hard to tell fact from fiction in a town dominated by legends of a defeated monster and a fairytale castle, set dramatically above the Rhône. The massive Renaissance castle, the centre of King René and Queen Jeanne's sumptuous court, is real enough, but the character Tartarin, who supposedly inhabited the 'house' on boulevard Itam, was the creation of Alphonse Daudet in his trilogy of *Prodigious Adventures*. As for the monster...according to legend, the *Tarasque* came from the Rhône and devoured local townsfolk until St Martha – who had arrived with the three Marys at Stes-Maries-de-la-Mer – ordered it to return to the river with the sign of the cross. The monster certainly lives again every June in a colourful procession through the streets, and St Martha is said to have been buried in the carved sarcophagus that can be seen in the crypt of the church later named for her.

# VAR & ALPES-DE-HAUTE-PROVENCE

This region is in fact two *départements* – Var and Alpes-de-Haute-Provence – the great and largely undiscovered heart of Provence between the better-known Bouches-du-Rhône and Vaucluse to the west and the glamorous Côte d'Azur further east. The scenery can be dramatic with coastal mountain ranges and Europe's deepest canyon, while the quiet inland towns remain much as they've been for centuries.

## THE VAR

Var has the longest coastline of Provence, highly populated in the west with the resorts of Bandol (famous for its red wines), Sanary-sur-Mer and the naval port of Toulon itself, one of the most underrated cities in Provence, with a maze of old streets and public transport by ferries as well as buses. Beyond the heights of Mont-Faron, which you can ascend by cable car to view the whole sweep of the bay, Toulon is backed by some impressive scenery: deep gorges and peaks hiding medieval villages such as Evenos and Ollioules, which invite you to leave the car and investigate on foot.

Though a peaceful inland backwater today, Hyères was the first winter resort in the South of France, particularly popular with English visitors. To the south, via a busy marina and working salt flats, a causeway has made the island of Giens a peninsula, one of the many places from which to take a ferry to the nearby Iles d'Hyères. The largest of this group of islands, Porquerolles and Port-Cros, remain wild and unspoilt, and can only be explored on foot or by bicycle.

**Côte d'Azur countryside near the village of Tourtour**

The rest of the Var coast is backed by two imposing forested mountain ranges, which suffer nearly every summer from devastating fires: in the centre, the vast and almost impenetrable Massif des Maures, and towards the east the smaller Massif de l'Esterel. Both offer stunning views from the Corniche roads cut into the coast between the mountains and the sea. The steep and twisty road that crosses the Massif des Maures leads to one of the Riviera's most famous names, St-Tropez – still tiny compared with its giant reputation, and surrounded by a cluster of ancient and fashionable villages.

All this lies south of the A8 autoroute known as *La Provençale*. The upper reaches of the Var have a distinct lack of main roads, and a network of handsome villages: the suggested motor tour from Aups takes in several of them, together with a restored Cistercian abbey and panoramic views.

## ALPES-DE-HAUTE-PROVENCE

The Alpes-de-Haute-Provence are altogether different and, arriving from the south, begin with the most spectacular landscape of the whole region, the Grand Canyon de Verdon. Its cliffs, riverbed and the Lac de Ste-Croix provide innumerable opportunities for adventure, whether your passion is for walking, rock climbing, canoeing or dramatic driving.

At the eastern end of the gorge, Castellane lies on the Route Napoléon, the path which the escaping emperor took from Elba back to Paris. North lies Digne-les-Bains – an elegant and remote spa town which is the northern terminus of the popular train, the Chemin de Fer de Provence – and Sisteron, whose former strategic importance is evident from its great fortifications. Further down the train line are Annot and Entrevaux, worth exploring on the way to Nice on the Côte d'Azur.

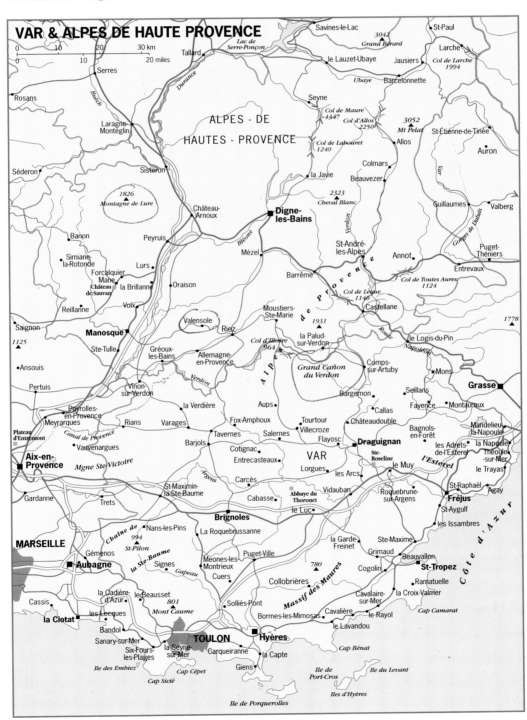

The agricultural village of Cotignac – one of the attractions of the Haut-Var, which enjoys a spectacular setting on a tufa cliff

## ALLOS

*MAP REF: 113 E3*

High in the Vallée du Verdon on the edge of the Parc National du Mercantour, Allos has been made accessible by its growth as a ski resort. In summer this is good walking country, particularly around the sizeable Lac d'Allos, a 13km tortuous drive via the D226 and then a 1km walk to the lake itself. There is a circular path right around the lake.

## ANNOT

*MAP REF: 113 E3*

Annot is a welcoming small town, inaccessible enough in the mountainous lower Alps to lie off the main tourist trail, but easily reached as a day trip from Nice on the Chemin de Fer de Provence (CFP) – the private railway that crosses the Alpes de Sud from Digne-les-Bains to Nice.

The surrounding sandstone hills, the Grès d'Annot, have provided homes here for over 2,000 years, first as troglodyte dwellings, later as building materials for the Renaissance quarter of the present town. The weird shapes of the eroded sandstone have long been a source of wonder.

The town moved to its present site on the River Vaïre from the original Roman settlement at Vers-la-Ville (see walk). The restored ancient pont de Réfuge leads to the Verimande quarter across the river, where the chapel of the

Knights Templar can still be seen.

Annot's old quarter lies to the north of the large square shaded by plane trees – narrow streets lined with equally narrow houses, the most notable being the Maison des Arcades built in 1675, which lead up to the church with its Renaissance bell tower.
**Nearby** There are several *grottes* (caves) open to the public at the towns of St-Benoit (6km east on the N202) and Méailles (10km north via the D908 and D210), both served by the Chemin de Fer de Provence. For more details, contact the tourist office in Annot, tel: 92 83 23 03.

## AUPS

*MAP REF: 113 D2*

Some 23km south of the Grand Canyon de Verdon, among the wooded hills of the Haut-Var, Aups is the northernmost town of a group of old communities that still rely mainly on agriculture rather than tourism. A search for the authentic has brought more and more visitors to this and the other Haut-Var villages, but they seem to have remained largely unspoiled.

Aups itself is one of the main market towns of the region, and is one of the best places to buy Provençal honey. The wrought-iron belfry, fountains and remains of ramparts are typical small-town Provence; the Simon-Ségal Museum of Modern Art, in the former Ursuline convent in rue Albert 1er, is less so.

## COUNTRY WALK

This circuit takes two and a half hours, of which about an hour is uphill, and passes most of the best-known rock formations including the Chambre du Roi. It is marked by blue triangles: to obtain more information before you start the walk, contact the Centre de Montagne et de Ski de Fond at Colle Basse, tel: 92 83 28 14.

*Starting in the main square in Annot, follow the avenue de la Gare past the station and climb for another 5 minutes to reach the old canal d'Arrosage and the first of the named rocks, Le Zodiaque.*

Like many of the rocks, the Zodiaque is popular with climbers – this one offering 12 climbs of varying difficulty. Opposite, the *blocs* also have graded climbs. Continuing on the path, you pass between the Bloc des Vaudois and Rochers du Visage, then the Rocher le Bestiaire, which is on the left, the Bloc d'Alrain, which is on the right, and Les Pyramides, opposite.

*About 45 minutes' walk after passing the station you should reach the grand cavern of the Chambre du Roi itself. From here the path begins to bear left across a plateau area before it eventually reaches the arches of les Portettes and the Defilé des Garambes, another 40 minutes on.*

You now begin a long descent through the wooded area known as Les Espaluns to the chapel of Notre-Dame at Vers-la-Ville – the site of the original Roman settlement here – from where there is a good view over Annot. The final descent, leading to the main square, takes about 10 minutes.

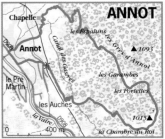

# MOTOR TOUR

Most of the villages in this 80km tour of the Haut-Var could be used as a base for exploring the area further.

*Leaving Aups on the D22, continue south for 9km, joining the Bresque valley to reach Sillans-la-Cascade.*

### Sillans-la-Cascade
This attractive small village seems to be going the same way as its long-abandoned ramparts, although only drought ever prevents the River Bresque from cascading near by. The waterfall is a short walk to the left from the road just past the village.

*Continue south for 6km on the D22 to Cotignac.*

### Cotignac
Like Aups, Cotignac is a large agricultural village, which spills from the vegetated slopes of a tufa cliff topped by a pair of ruined towers. The natural backdrop of the cliff is full of interconnected caves; to explore them further, follow the path from the church. In summer the picturesque streets are animated by an open-air theatre festival.

Just as you leave the village to the south, a narrow lane to the right climbs to the 16th-century chapel of Notre-Dame de Grâces, with views south to Carcès.

*Return to the D13 and continue south for 7km through Carcès. Following signs for Cabasse, you reach a series of cascades before the shores of the Lac de Carcès.*

### Lac de Carcès
If you want to explore the lake further, cross the bridge at the southern end (towards Brignoles) and follow the footpath along the west shore.

*After 2km on the D13, turn left and drive through bauxite country and the Forêt de la Darboussière to the Abbaye du Thoronet.*

### Abbaye du Thoronet
Le Thoronet was the earliest and 'purest' of the three Cistercian abbeys founded in Provence in the 12th century, Sénanque and Silvacane being the other two, and still reflects the simplicity and harmony of its foundation.

*Continue on the D79, turning left at the junction with the D84;*

*after 4km cross the River Argens and turn left on to the D562. The next two right turnings lead to Entrecasteaux; the second option offers much better driving conditions.*

### Entrecasteaux
This tiny medieval village is of particular interest to horticulture enthusiasts, as its imposing public gardens were laid out by Versaille's landscaper, André le Nôtre. Even more impressive is the castle which lies beyond the gardens: after early days of grandeur entertaining such notables as Madame de Sévigné, the château was in ruins until its rescue in the 1970s by Scot Ian McGarvie-Munn.

*Follow the Bresque 8km north on the D31 to Salernes. Take the road northeast to Villecroze (two alternatives).*

### Villecroze
Nestling in wooded limestone hills riddled with more caves, Villecroze also has an impressive municipal park. A guided tour of the caves takes you into many that were used as hide-outs and dwellings. The old village has a medieval clock tower, doorways

and arcades (rue des Arceaux). The weekly market is held on Thursday mornings in the place du Village and a *brocante* (not quite antique) fair is held on the first Sunday in May and last Sunday in August.

*For views across the region in all directions, stop 1km along the D51 to Tourtour, at the belvedere and orientation table. At the junction with the D77 turn right for the journey to Tourtour.*

### Tourtour
There are more views from this pretty village. Neolithic remains have been found near by, and geologists will enjoy the extensive fossil collection at the Maison Communale d'Exposition.

Tourtour was the original site of the Cistercian abbey before the monks moved to Le Thoronet. The 12th-century Tour du Grimaud still stands, as do two of the elms planted to commemorate the visit of Anne of Austria in 1638. The best views can be had from the church of St-Denis, which is on the south side of Tourtour.

*Return to Aups via the D77.*

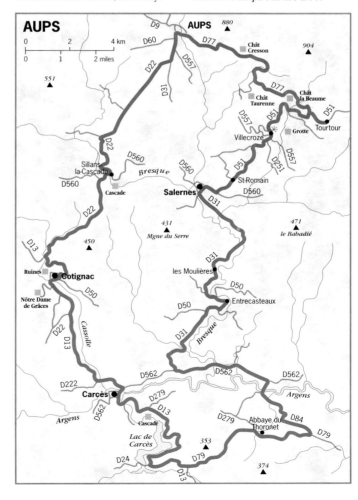

## BANDOL

*MAP REF: 112 C1*

Bandol is a resort in the best tradition of the South of France. It trades under the slogan *un style à vivre*: the requisite Côte backdrop of a marina and casino are here, together with good beaches and elegant 19th-century villas. There are also opportunities to try a huge variety of sporting activities, guided walks, and, of course, the local wine.

Bandol's red wines are some of the region's best; when you have tried a bottle from the Maison du Vin on the allées Vivien, or from the *caves* (cellars) in the rue de la République, pick up a list of the 50 local *domaines* and châteaux that welcome visitors (see **Nearby**).

The morning market sets up in place de la Liberté, where you can buy items for a picnic lunch before taking one of the short and frequent boat trips to the Ile de Bendor. Owned by Paul Ricard (of *pastis* and motor circuit fame), this small island is a commercial entity in its own right, with three hotels, a conference centre and an international diving school. Behind the small beach are the Exposition Universelle des Vins et Spiritueux, the Musée de la Mer and the Fondation Paul Ricard, an art gallery that also runs instructional courses.

The beach most favoured by the locals is Bandol's deep, sandy bay of Renecros, west of the marina via boulevard Lumière. From here

you can follow the 11km Sentier Littoral, or coastal path, west to La Madrague de St-Cyr via the Calanque du Port d'Alon.

**For history buffs** Near the port of La Madrague, which is also accessible by car from St-Cyr or les Lecques, you can visit a museum featuring the remains of the Roman villa of *Tauroentum*.

**Back to nature** The Gros Cerveau (reached by car most easily from Ollioules – see page 70) can be explored on foot from Bandol. Follow signs to the Jardin Exotique and Zoo (worth visiting), turning right off the D559b to Le Beausset, under the autoroute intersection and left again after 1km. The path starts opposite the chapel of St-Ternide, climbing up through the vines and branching right to join the route des Crêtes. To the left the pointe du Cerveau offers magnificent views across the coast and the Grès de Ste-Anne. To follow a circular route, continue east and take the next descending path to return to the chapel.

**Nearby** Inland, the hill town of La Cadière d'Azur is at the centre of Bandol wine production, with about 20 *domaines* open to visitors between here and Le Plan-du-Castellet. From the streets of the old town there are views north to the smaller fortified village of Le Castellet, near the Ricard Grand Prix circuit. Above the small town of Le Beausset, the restored Romanesque chapel of Notre-Dame du Beausset-Vieux commands a panoramic view of the area.

## BARCELONETTE

*MAP REF: 113 E4*

The northwest corner of the Alpes-de-Haute-Provence reveals a stunning landscape, and presents a challenge to any enthusiastic motorist, with some of the highest and twistiest roads in Europe. The main town of this corner of Provence is worthy of its dramatic approach, though it can more easily be reached via the D900 *star* from the Lac de Serre-Ponçon. The town of Barcelonette, which was founded during the 13th century by the counts of Provence – who were also the counts of Barcelona – is today an elegant and peaceful place.

The magnificent mansions on avenue de la Libération belie the Mexican influence on their 19th-century builders, many of whom had made their fortunes there before returning to France. Mexican and Indian art is displayed alongside the tools of more traditional Provençal crafts and professions at the Musée de la Vallée de l'Ubaye, at 10 avenue de la Libération, open daily.

**Nearby** An excellent base for exploring, Barcelonette lies at the centre of a popular skiing area, with resorts based at Pra-Loup, Le Sauze and Super-Sauze and also in the upper reaches of the Parc National du Mercantour (see page 105).

**The good life is celebrated in style by visitors to Bandol, an elegant Côte d'Azur resort**

## BARJOLS
*MAP REF: 113 D2*

Barjols, set in lush, fruit-growing countryside, is best-known for a bizarre celebration with medieval origins. The Fête de St-Marcel in January celebrates the burial of a local saint in 1350 with a musical procession through the streets, followed by the slaughter of a cow and its consumption, once roasted, by the local townsfolk. The rest of the year, look out for the many artisans' workshops, as Barjols was for many years the traditional centre of musical instrument manufacture, including the Provençal flute, the *galoubet*.
**Nearby** The verdant landscape is laced with streams and rivers, and the source of one, the Argens, can be found 15km to the southwest via the pretty Vallon de Font-Taillarde. To the southeast, follow the Eau Salée and branch left at Châteauvert to follow the more sober Vallon de Sourn to the pretty village of Correns, which, like nearby Montfort-sur-Argens, has a castle.

## BORMES-LES-MIMOSAS
*MAP REF: 113 D1*

This Provençal village, just 5km inland from Le Lavandou, is almost too good to be true. But even if the yellow-flowering Mimosa trees themselves haven't been here for hundreds of years, the castle at the centre of the blossom-laden pathways is genuine enough. The renovated houses along steep, flower-filled streets have made it popular with artists, and some of their predecessors' work can be seen in the regional museum in rue Carnot. The twisting D41 climbs into the Massif des Maures

behind the village through the Col de Gratteloup, offering some spectacular views back down to the coast.

## BRIGNOLES SAT MARKET
*MAP REF: 113 D2*

Lying just off the Autoroute La Provençale halfway between Toulon's busy coast and the peace of the Lac Ste-Croix, Brignoles is a large town which combines the two faces of the Var: a modern town spawned by the bauxite mining industry, spreading out below a hillside medieval quarter. As well as industrial raw materials, the local land has also long produced marble, and soft fruits, especially plums and peaches, and wine.

Everything of immediate interest is in the old quarter: from place Carami, stepped alleyways lead to the church of St-Sauveur, whose greatest treasure is a 17th-century *Descent from the Cross* by local artist Parrocel. Rue des Lanciers's ancient houses lead to the place des Comtes de Provence and the former home of the medieval counts of Provence, now housing the Musée du Pays Brignolais. The collection of regional art and anthropology is a good opportunity to gain an insight into the locality, and includes the castle chapel, a reconstructed kitchen, and a cement boat, made by Brignoles' own inventor of reinforced concrete.
**For children** You can visit most of France's best-known sights in one day – and all at your kids' height – at the Parc Minifrance, 7km east of Brignoles on the N7.

**A fisherman works while others play at the resort of Bandol**

**Red-roofed houses hug the hillside at Bormes-les-Mimosas, a perfect Provençal village**

**Nearby** Brignoles would make an alternative base for a tour of the Haut-Var villages (see page 61), starting from Carcès, which is 17km northeast on the D562 via le Val. To reach the southern end of the pretty Lac de Carcès, follow the River Carami on the D24, passing the château and village of Vins-sur-Carami and the perched chapel of St-Vincent. For the best view, turn left immediately before the lake and climb the narrow lane. A footpath follows the west side of the lake past the dam and the waterfalls and continues to Carcès. About 5km south of the lake, the village of Cabasse has an interesting 16th-century church.

## CASTELLANE

*MAP REF: 113 E3*

Castellane's tourist brochures can make this appear a sizeable, bustling place where lively shopping streets vie for your attention with a rich cultural heritage. Castellane is, however, relatively small – though Napoleon did stop here *en route* to Paris (see box), and on Wednesday and Saturday mornings the main place Marcel Sauvaire is as busy as any Provençal market town.

The town is compact, but has all the necessary amenities for exploring the spectacular Gorges du Verdon, near by. Several companies offer activities in and around the water of the canyon, from rafting, canyoning and abseiling to 'The Great Thrill' of jumping from a great height supported only by a bunji, or elasticated rope. Most of the companies stress the presence of trained instructors.

Those more interested in shooting the scenery than the rapids might like to visit the summer exhibition of the Photo-Club Castellanais, open Tuesday, Thursday and Saturday afternoons at the Eglise St-Victor.

Apart from the sporting and camping facilities, historic interest lies largely above the town, dominated as it is by a gigantic limestone rock, topped by the little chapel of Notre-Dame-du-Roc dating from 1703.

**For children** Adventurous children with less enthusiastic parents can still enjoy canoeing or windsurfing on the Lac de Castillon, north of the town. Four- to 14 year-olds can join a programme of activities under the supervision of the Centre Aéré; details from rue du 11-Novembre or the tourist information office, who also have details of boat hire on the lake and excursions in the gorge itself.

**Back to nature** If the roads are not too crowded, the spectacular views make a tour of the gorge a memorable experience. The Gorges du Verdon is home to a wide range of wildlife and the best way for experienced hikers to see it on foot is to follow the Sentier Martel (GR4), 14km long and taking about 8 hours. It starts at the Chalet de la Maline on the D23 and is signed with red and white markers. Go well-equipped, with boots, extra clothes, a torch for the tunnels, and water.

**Nearby** Northwest of Castellane the Lac de Castillon provides a gentler landscape as well as easier ways to take to the water. The most dramatic sight is the Barrage de Castillon, an enormous and intimidating concrete dam. The road hugs the shoreline, crossing the River Rioul at St-Julien-du-Verdon, from where the steep Clue de Vergons leads west to Annot (see page 60) and crosses the lake at the Pont St-Julien, 4km south of the small alpine resort of St-André-les-Alpes. From here the scenic D202 leads west to Barrême, from where you can return to Castellane via the D85.

## CHATEAU-ARNOUX

*MAP REF: 113 D3*

Sandwiched between the autoroute and a stretch of the Durance where it forms the Lac de l'Escale, this busy town is dominated by a mighty Renaissance castle. Built in the early 16th century by Pierre de Glandêves, its five towers – square, round and hexagonal – stand in a peaceful moment. Inside, the carved stone staircase is the best feature. For a panorama of the whole area, climb or drive to the belvedere of the Chapelle St-Jean at the summit of the hill of St-Jean, approached off the N96 south to St-Auban.

Across the lake from Château-Arnoux, Volonne is a pretty village with its own fortified remains. The ruined towers on the hill date from the early 11th century and the church of St-Martin is a contemporary building. Napoleon stopped here on his way north from Elba.

**Nearby** There are several ruined châteaux along the Route Napoléon as it branches east along the Bléone river, past the mysterious rock formations known as the Pénitents des Mées.

## ROUTE NAPOLEON

After escaping from the island of Elba, Napoleon landed at Golfe-Juan on 1 March and set off with troops to reclaim Paris. His route was roughly equivalent to today's N85, now known as the Route Napoléon and clearly marked, as are several of the places where he stopped on the way.

A plaque and bust at Golfe-Juan mark the landing and start of his journey. His route took him through Cannes, Mouans-Sartoux, Grasse, St-Vallier-de-Thiey, Escragnolles, and Castellane, where the troops crossed the Verdon by the now disused stone bridge. After Barrême, he marched north to Digne before reaching Malijai in only three days. On 5 March he continued north to Volonne and Sisteron, eventually reaching Paris via Grenoble and Lyon.

The Gorges du Verdon offers a range of activities and natural beauty to take your breath away

# MOTOR TOUR

At the height of summer a tour of the Gorges du Verdon can be a slow and frustrating procession of cars and coaches along one of Europe's most dramatic, and treacherous roads. If you plan to make the whole circuit from Castellane (over 130km) allow at least 4 hours, which will permit several stops *en route* at the signed viewpoints, as well as a short visit to Moustiers (see page 70). If you find the prospect of driving along the edge of the precipice less than thrilling, be sure to follow the tour in the suggested anti-clockwise direction.

*From Castellane take the D952 (to Moustiers) and follow the Verdon for 12km through the Clue de Chasteuil to the Pont de Soleils. Continue on the D952 through the Clue de Carejuan to enter the canyon proper; immediately after the second short tunnel a road branches down to the left to the Couloir Samson (tunnel) – the end of the Sentier Martel at the confluence of the River Verdon and the Baou.*

## Point Sublime
The Point Sublime here is the first main viewpoint; for an even higher view turn right on to the narrow D17 to the village of Rougon, dominated by the ruins of a feudal fortress.

*About 6km further, almost at La Palud-sur-Verdon, the Route des Crêtes turns off to the left to provide a series of spectacular viewpoints over the Verdon. The chalet de la Maline marks the other end of the Sentier Martel.*

## La Palud
A hair-raising 23km later you rejoin the D952 at the village of La Palud, less than 2km from where you left it. The largest village on the northern side of the canyon, it has an attractive church and a couple of hotels and cafés, as well as several more rafting and riding companies, and is a good alternative to Castellane if you plan to spend several days exploring the gorge.

*Another 17.5km further, via the great hairpin bends of the Belvédère de Mayreste and the Belvédère du Galetas, the road divides north to Moustiers and south for the south side of the canyon, the Corniche Sublime.*

## Lac de Ste-Croix
This west end of the canyon is dominated by the Lac de Ste-Croix, and the view from the Pont du Galetas, where the river opens out to a vast expanse of water, is one of the most breathtaking. To experience it at its most dramatic, hire pedaloes from the sandy

**You must brave the crowds and a hair-raising drive to enjoy the Verdon scenery**

beach and wend your way between the towering cliffs.

*Turn left on to the D19 for the climb up to Aiguines.*

## Aiguines
Through the tunnel of the Col d'Illoire the next landmarks are the Cirque de Vaumale and the Falaise des Cavaliers, and another series of spectacular viewpoints, including the Balcons de la Mescla (park and walk a short distance), the last view of the river before the road leaves the Verdon.

*Four kilometres past le Petit-St-Maymes turn left to Trigance. At the D955 turn left to cross the Pont de Soleils and rejoin the D952 to Castellane. Alternatively turn south to Jabron, which can also be reached via the village of Comps-sur-Artuby, and follow the narrow and remote D52 back to Castellane.*

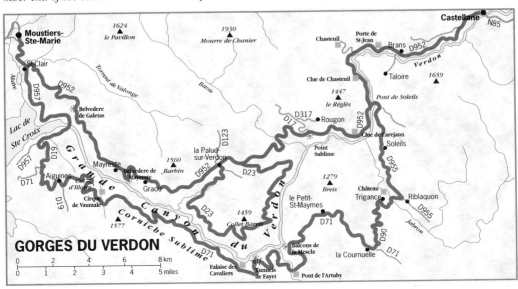

**GORGES DU VERDON**

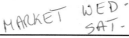

## COLMARS-LES-ALPES
*MAP REF: 113 E3*

The strategic importance of mountain passes in the 17th century is still apparent today where the twisting road from the Col des Champs joins the road along the Vallée du Haut-Verdon. The lands to the east were then part of a rival state, the Duchy of Savoy, and Louis XIV's so-called *corset de forteresses* (sic) was planned to stretch from Briançon in the north to Entrevaux in the south via Embrun, Seyne and Colmars. The defensive walls and the forts of Savoie (to the east) and France add to the charm of this village today. If you want a better insight into local history, visit the Collection d'Art et d'Histoire at the Porte de Savoie, open afternoons only, in July and August.

Like nearby Allos (see page 60), this area of Provence is excellent hiking country. Follow the River Lance up to the Pont Mission, where there are waterfalls and a superb view over Colmars; or alternatively explore the attractive villages of Bas- and Haut-Chaumie via the Forêt de Colmars to the north.

**The cathedral at Dignes-les-Bains, set in the heart of the 'new' (that is, medieval) part of town**

## DIGNE-LES-BAINS
*MAP REF: 113 D3*

The northern terminus of the Chemin de Fer de la Provence is the elegant spa town and departmental capital of the Alpes-de-Haute-Provence. It's a quiet place with a remote feel, which comes alive during the annual August lavender market and its other festivals. Several of its more interesting features are on the edge of town, including the thermal baths, fed by the *Eaux Chaudes* to the southeast and the fascinating Fondation Alexandra David-Neel, a Tibetan cultural centre established at Samten Dzong, once the home of the writer. To the northeast of the town centre, the 13th-century former cathedral of Notre-Dame du Bourg is arguably more inspiring than the present cathedral of St-Jérôme, in the medieval 'new town'.

From here, boulevard Gassendi, scene of Digne's many markets, leads to the Municipal Museum specialising in the archaeology of Upper Provence, and the aptly named Fontaine-Grande.

**Back to nature** The Cordeliers Botanical Garden at the Maria Borély College has over 350 plants laid out in a medieval *carreaux* design, with four squares, devoted, respectively, to a flower garden, a fruit garden, a vegetable garden and a garden of medicinal plants.

**Nearby** Digne stands at the heart of the Réserve Géologique de Haute-Provence, the largest geological reserve in Europe, although access to see the rare collection of fossils is strictly limited. Contact the Centre Géologique at the Domaine St-Benoît, (tel: 92 31 51 31).

The particularly difficult 6km drive north to the Romanesque church at Courbons is rewarded with great views across the town, with another panorama to be enjoyed from the ruined Chapelle de la Croix above Notre-Dame du Bourg.

### FESTIVALS AT DIGNE

Throughout the year, and in summer in particular, Digne is host to a wide variety of arts festivals. For a full list of what's on when you plan to visit, contact the departmental tourist office (see page 117). Annual events include a film festival, Cinéma d'Eté, in April, an International Sculpture Symposium and Chansons de la Provence in July, a feminist film festival in late September and an International Accordion Festival in October.

## DRAGUIGNAN

*MAP REF: 113 D2*

Although it no longer has the status of department capital, Draguignan still has the feel of a town at ease with its own prosperity. Along broad avenues, municipal buildings include the *sous-préfecture*, Palais de Justice and theatre, behind which stands an interesting museum with a mixture of decorative and fine arts, but more picturesque by far are the place du Marché and the old quarter, which, centring on the Tour de l'Horloge, is still guarded by the medieval gateways, the Porte Aiguières and the Porte Romaine.

**Nearby** Draguignan lies just to the south of the vast military training ground of Canjuers. On boulevard John Kennedy, to the west of town, the Cimetière Américain commemorates the Allied landings of 1944.

Five kilometres south, in Trans-en-Provence, the River Nartuby flows through the town in a series of cascades. The town also has a particularly elegant Hôtel de Ville and a curious *puits aérien*, shaped like a modern *borie*, and designed as an experiment to trap atmospheric humidity.

Some 12km south of Draguignan, in Côte-de-Provence wine country, the small village of Les Arcs lies just to the east of the villages described in the motor tour from Aups (see page 61). Like them, it has a picturesque restored old quarter, topped with the keep of a ruined 12th-century castle. Four kilometres northeast on the D91, the cloister and chapel of Ste-Roseline are all that remain of a Romanesque abbey named after the 14th-century saint who is buried here.

## ENTREVAUX

*MAP REF: 113 E3*

The name of Entrevaux is inextricably linked with that of Vauban, Louis XIV's military architect, responsible for so many of France's most impressive forts. Here, the fortress is perched way above the small town, linked by a mighty zig-zagging ramp, while the town itself is saved from spilling into the river by a ring of ramparts.

You must explore the town of Entrevaux on foot, crossing the Pont-Levis and entering via the remarkable Porte Royale, which houses the Acceuil (information office) together with an exhibition showing a model of the town and a collection of *santons*. To go straight to the entry to the citadel,

**Draguignan's Tour de l'Horloge**

bear left to find rue de l'Orbitelle across from place St-Martin and past the Porte de France; allow half an hour for the stiff climb. On the opposite side of town follow rue du Marché past the fountain and the tiny clock tower that straddles rue de l'Horloge to rue de l'Eglise and the cathedral, whose southern side is incorporated into the defensive walls.

Those interested in a more contemporary technology can visit a collection of over 60 motor-cycles at the Musée de la Moto in rue Haute, while every August, the townsfolk of Entrevaux don medieval costume for the *journées médiévales* and the streets are full of fire-eaters, tumblers and troubadours.

Entrevaux is also served by the trains of the Chemin de Fer de la Provence and the Train des Pignes, whose station is a short way along the N202 to the east. For the best views of the town and its fortress, drive up the small winding lane opposite the Porte Royale, which climbs above the town cemetery.

**For children** Outside the walls beneath the cathedral are the town football pitch and tennis courts, together with a children's adventure play area. You can leave the town via the remarkable wooden construction of the third gate, the Porte d'Italie.

## FAYENCE

*MAP REF: 113 E2*

This large, attractive village is the hub of a series of picturesque villages on the plains northeast of Draguignan. The narrow streets of the old town, protected by the 14th-century Saracen's Gate, climb up to an 18th-century church and clock tower. From the terrace next to the church you can see the gliders' aerodrome below, and the Massif de l'Esterel beyond.

**For history buffs** To reach the exceptionally pretty village of Mons, to the north, you could detour via the tortuous D37 and D56 to pass the Roman aqueduct at Roche Taillée, built to supply Fréjus.

**Nearby** Within walking distance are the village of Tourettes and the Romanesque chapel of Notre-Dame-des-Cyprès, while beyond lies a succession of beautiful, largely unspoilt villages which could detain you for days. To the east are Callian and Montauroux, from where you can see the Lac de St-Cassien, 6km further south. To the west, on the road to Seillans, once home to artist Max Ernst, is another Romanesque chapel, Notre-Dame-de-l'Ormeau, which has a superb Renaissance altarpiece depicting the visit of the shepherds and the adoration of the Magi, while 13km further west lies elegant Bargemon, once fortified, and now shaded by plane trees.

*[handwritten annotations: MONDAY MARKET; MARKET SAT; WALK ENR ST TROPEZ]*

## FORCALQUIER
*MAP REF: 112 C3*

Forcalquier's attractive streets
have a faded look, and at first
there is little to suggest that this
town was once one of the most
powerful in Provence. There are
good views from the church of
Notre-Dame-de-Provence, summer
concerts and exhibitions in the
former Convent of the Cordeliers,
and local archaeology, arts and
crafts in the Musée Municipal, on
place du Bourguet. To the north of
the town, an elegant cemetery has
arcades of clipped yew.
**Nearby** There is even more to see
around Forcalquier, including the
Barrage de la Laye (D13 from
Mane), the Romanesque church of
Notre-Dame-de-Salagon and the
classical 18th-century Château de
Sauvan, also south of Mane, which
stands at the centre of a triangle of
attractive villages. About 8km to
the south, off the D13, lies
Dauphin; 11km to the east is
medieval Lurs, from where you
can also visit the superb mosaics at
the Prieuré de Ganagobie, and
west is the village of Simiane-la-
Rotonde, with its curious ruined
castle. Simiane is 22km from St-
Michel de l'Observatoire and the
Observatoire de Haute-Provence;
to make a round trip, return to
Forcalquier via the D950 and
Banon, known for its goats'
cheese. A 4km footpath from
Banon leads to the Gouffre du
Caladaire.

## FRÉJUS
*MAP REF: 113 E2*

Fréjus, like many inland towns, has
a coastal outpost, Fréjus-Plage, but
it is the heart of the town that
anyone interested in Roman and
medieval Provence should seek
out. In the first century BC *Forum
Julii* was a port and an important
naval base until the harbour silted
up. Roman remains include the
amphitheatre, still in use today,
the Porte des Gaules, Butte St-
Antoine, Porte d'Orée, Lanterne
d'Auguste, the quay of the former
port, and the theatre.
   A map of the city will show the
relationship of the present streets
and buildings to the Roman town.
Most noticeable in the current
landscape is the remarkable
medieval ensemble of the fortified
cathedral close or *Cité Episcopale*.
It includes one of the oldest
baptisteries in France, the
cathedral of Notre-Dame and a
beautiful 12th-century cloister,
together with an archaeological
museum which displays some of
the many Roman relics found in
the city.
**For history buffs** Outside the town,
on the route de Bagnols-en-Forêt,
the Musée des Troupes de Marine
illustrates the history and battles of
the French Marines from their
formation in the early 17th
century.

**Forcalquier, once a force to be
reckoned with in Provence**

## GARDE-FREINET, LA
*MAP REF: 113 E2*

On the winding, picturesque road
that crosses the Massif des
Maures, the village of La Garde-
Freinet stands over 400m above
sea level; its ruined fortress to the
north was one of the last Moorish
strongholds in Provence. A
footpath from the road to Roches
Blanches (another good
viewpoint) leads up to the ruins.
The attractive village celebrates a
number of fêtes and festivals,
including the *Fête de la Forêt des
Maures* in mid-June and the *Fête
du Hameau de la Moure* two
months later. All year round you
can see crafts and local produce
for sale at the Maison de La Garde-
Freinet on the Grimaud road.

## GIENS
*MAP REF: 113 D1*

As one of the Iles d'Hyères, Giens
would have been closer to
Porquerolles than to the
mainland, but it has long been a
*presqu'île* (peninsula), attached
by two causeways just south of
Toulon-Hyères airport. The lagoon
between the two, the Salins des
Pesquiers, still has working salt
flats. The route de la Capte faces
east, as do the long sandy beaches
of La Capte and Hyères-Plage. In
the village of Giens the mound of
the former castle is the best local
viewpoint.
   At the southeast tip of the
peninsula, La Tour Fondue,
currently being restored, stands
next to a small *gare maritime*.
From here boats make the
shortest crossing to Porquerolles,
the largest of the Iles d'Hyères,
and also do tours of all three
islands. Some of the boats are
catamarans with underwater glass
sides. There is a series of small
sandy beaches near the tower,
accessible on foot.

## GRIMAUD
*MAP REF: 113 E2*

This ancient village perches on
the edge of the Massif des Maures,
6km from the Golfe de St-Tropez
and 10km south of La Garde-
Freinet. Pretty, restored streets
climb up to the Romanesque
church of St-Michel and the
ruined castle, once ruled over by
the Grimaldi family, from whose
name Grimaud derives.
**Nearby** At the head of the Golfe
de St-Tropez, Port-Grimaud basks
in its own perfection. In this
pastiche Provençal village created
in the 1960s, you need a boat –
preferably a large yacht – to reach

*[vertical text in left margin]* • FORCALQUIER

68

your front door. To the south of Grimaud, the attractive town of Cogolin is famous for its hand-made pipes, carpets (and museum), furniture and reeds for wind instruments, as well as for its wine.

## HYÈRES
### MAP REF: 113 D1

Hyères was the first resort of the French Riviera and popular with English visitors, including Queen Victoria, even before Nice and Cannes. It claims that it was here, in 1887, that Stephen Liégeard, author of that influential 19th-century book, first coined the phrase *Côte d'Azur*. Despite its reputation for palm trees, mild climate and elegant villas, don't be surprised to find that it lies 4km from the sea – the main reason for the historic old quarter having survived remarkably intact.

Today it is old Hyères which is most intriguing. Above the broad avenues of the lower town, the elegant gardens of the Hôtel de Ville and the Casino, the 13th-century Porte Massillon leads up to the hub of the Vieille Ville, the place Massillon, where the daily market is watched over by the Tour St-Blaise, part of a Templar commandery built around 1200.

Rue Ste-Catherine climbs up further, to the place St-Paul in front of the church with its Romanesque belfry, and to the Porte Barbacane, a gateway under the turret of a Renaissance house. An orientation table points out the main features of the view from the terrace. In rue Ste-Claire you can see the Gothic Porte des Princes, and there is a Romanesque house in rue Paradis, which leads up to the Parc St-Bernard and, further up, the ruined château.

To the east of the town, off the place de la République, St-Louis is a sombre 13th-century church, in stark contrast with the very modern Notre-Dame de Con-solation, built in the 1950s to replace an 11th-century chapel.

Hyères' famous palm trees were first introduced from the Canary Isles in 1864 by the Comte Vigier, a keen amateur horticulturalist. The town became the palm tree capital, supplying them as far afield as Germany and Belgium, with more than 1,250,000 trees grown every year at its peak in the early 1920s. Before the arrival of the palm, the Hyères region was known for its violets and narcissi, which, with the arrival of the railway in 1882, could be transported to Paris.

Hyères' beaches stretch east and

**A ready-made resort: Port-Grimaud**

west and include the peninsula of Giens. The main resorts are Hyères-Plage (from where ferries depart for the Iles d'Hyères) and Ayguade-Ceinturon, but the small port of Les Salins, known locally as Les Vieux Salins, is prettier.

## ILES D'HYERES
### MAP REF: 113 D1

From almost any port between Toulon and Cavalaire-sur-Mer you can take a ferry to Var's group of islands, known variously as the Iles d'Hyères and the Iles d'Or. Of the three largest, the Ile du Levant is nearly completely occupied by the military, leaving Porquerolles and Port-Cros still with plenty of room to find some peace and quiet, thanks mainly to their protected status – Porquerolles is a Parc Domanial and Port-Cros is a Parc National (see page 72).

All the islands have been occupied for centuries (although Port-Cros today is virtually uninhabited) and both bear witness to their strategic importance with a series of fortresses, some dating from the 16th century, others more recently built by the Germans as defence batteries during World War II.

## LAVANDOU, LE
### MAP REF: 113 D1

Le Lavandou, lying at the western end of the Corniche des Maures and 5km from inland Bormes-les-Mimosas, successfully combines the role of fishing port with that of popular resort. Its main attribute for visitors is a broad, sandy beach. What the town may lack in charm it makes up for with facilities, particularly restaurants and shops – which obviously expect a wealthy clientele.

Boats leave regularly from the port for the Ile de Port-Cros and Ile du Levant (see page 72), both of which you can see from the shore. There are several good walks near by to suit all levels and ambition, including the headland of Cap Bénat to the southwest. Ask at the tourist office for details.

## MANOSQUE
### MAP REF: 112 C3

SAT MARKET

Between the eastern end of the Lubéron Mountains and the Durance valley and its autoroute, Manosque is at the heart of both ancient and modern Provence. The modern face is largely industrial, capitalising on good communications and the established EDF power stations and Nuclear Research Centre at Cadarache – a far cry from the landscape described by local writer Jean Giono. Souvenirs of the writer can be seen at the Exposition Giono in the Bibliothèque, rue Mont d'Or.

Manosque has a more typical Provençal face in its old quarter beyond the Porte Saunerie, where lively rather than picturesque streets and squares lead off the main shopping street, rue-Grande, particularly busy on market days.

The two central churches are St-Sauveur, which has a distinctive wrought-iron belfry, and Notre-Dame-de-Romigier, with a Romanesque doorway and 12th-century black Virgin. In the summer there is plenty of festive distraction, including a jazz festival in late July. There are good views from the chapel of St-Pancrace, at the summit of the Mont Toute Aures, southwest of the town centre.

**Nearby** Thirteen kilometres southeast of Manosque in the Verdon valley, Gréoux-les-Bains is an ancient and prosperous small spa town with a ruined castle that lies on the GR4 long-distance footpath. There are views of the reservoir upstream from the Barrage de Gréoux, and you can reach the château on the banks at

Esparron-du-Verdon, but the Basses Gorges du Verdon are more difficult to reach if you are travelling by car.

## MOUSTIERS-STE-MARIE
### MAP REF: 113 D3

MARKET FRI.

A spectacular setting and world-famous pottery have combined to leave this tiny village and its approach roads at the western end of the Gorges du Verdon heaving with tourists every summer.

Perched above the mottled, tiled rooftops, the chapel of Notre-Dame-de-Beauvoir dates from the 12th century and can be reached by a steep zig-zagging path; above that a bizarre star is suspended between the cliffs from a 227m-long chain. It is no longer the original; the first one was said to have been put there in the 12th century by a Chevalier de Blacas, who vowed to hang a star near the chapel if he managed to escape imprisonment alive.

A tumbling stream pours down from the rocks and through an attractive man-made ravine, formed by the overhanging houses and the church *place*. Beneath its elegant Romanesque bell tower, the church itself is a cool sanctuary on baking-hot days, with some interesting carved pews and a glass panel in the floor where you can see the rushing water beneath.

**A rooftop view of Moustiers-Ste-Marie**

## OLLIOULES
### MAP REF: 113 D1

Set in magnificent scenery 6km northwest of Toulon, the medieval town of Ollioules is best known for its cut-flower market – not the usual picturesque buckets of carnations and roses in the main square, but an enormous modern complex on the edge of town. The *Marché Floral Méditerranéen* is the biggest in France and, except for a couple of horticultural fairs such as the *Floralies Méditerranéenes* and *Horti-Azur*, strictly wholesale; most of the day's business is complete by 9am.

Above this fertile countryside rise the stark hills of the Gros Cerveau, which make for challenging driving rewarded by excellent views south across to the coast and north to the Grès de Ste-Anne (take the D20 from Ollioules), while to the northeast the Gorges d'Ollioules are best explored on foot.

The small town itself has plenty to see: the main square, place Jean-Jaurès, is dominated by the elegant *mairie* and the tower of the church of St-Laurent, whose fortress-like façade looks on to place Duprat. Inside, the church is equally austere, though there is a fine white marble angel and Virgin by Puget. St-Laurent is the town's patron saint and his feast is celebrated in the second week of August with a procession and fireworks.

Opposite the church, the arcaded rue Pierre et Marie Curie is the town's most picturesque street. From here, climb rue St-Laurent to place du Trémaillon where, looking north, there is a good view of the ruined 11th-century castle. Back down the hill, in rue Roger Salengro, an old olive-oil press has been carefully restored and is now used as an exhibition centre.

**For history buffs** Crossing the River Reppe via the ancient Pont Bonnefort leads past a ruined chapel to the Oppidum de la Courtine, site of a Celto-Ligurian settlement – first discovered in 1909, and the only one to be found so far in western Provence.

**Nearby** On the drive northwest on the N8 through the gorges, several narrow, winding roads lead up to the dramatic tiny village of Evenos, the easiest approach being the D462 from Ste-Anne d'Evenos, through the Vallée de Cimai. Views from the ruined castle are superb, but even more spectacular are those from the 801m Mont Caume (continue on the D462 through the village of Le Broussan and turn left at the Col du Corps de Garde).

# COUNTRY WALK

Allow four hours and wear strong shoes for this adventurous hike from Ollioules, which includes some climbing and gives a closer look at the Gorges d'Ollioules.

*Park on the N8 (the Route des Gorges) 2km north of the town, opposite the Club Canin. To the right of the road, a yellow dotted arrow marks the start of the footpath which crosses the bed of the usually dry River Reppe.*

After 500m the River Destel branches off to the right and the path follows it into the gorges. The ground is rocky and in places very slippery as smaller streams join the Destel. High above is the Château du Diable (Devil's Castle, 343m), while the path itself negotiates the Toboggan with the help of a cable.

*The yellow-marked path divides. To the right, away from the Destel, is an easier and shorter route, with the Fontaine des Joncs on the right; it rejoins the main path after about 20 minutes. The main Destel path itself continues via a recently created footpath within the narrow gorge, and branches right again (marked with a* trait jaune *– yellow line) to offer dramatic*

*views of the village of Evenos high above and the Gros Cerveau before it begins its descent south towards Ollioules.*

The path joins the blue path and turns right (left leads to Le Revest, see Toulon, **Nearby,** page 82), offering views across to Ste-Baume and the sea. The path follows a valley looping below the Château du Diable rock. At the Col-du-Télégraph, turn right again onto the *trait jaune* which has come from Châteauvallon; the blue path continues past a ruined chapel to Ollioules itself. Crossing the Barre de Taillan, the path descends quickly with some good views across to Ollioules, back to the Reppe and the start of the walk. Just before the end, the path passes Le Mascaron, a spring where the water has been measured at 23˚C.

**Evenos, a village set above the Gros Cerveau**

### *PORQUEROLLES*
#### *MAP REF: 113 D1*

The largest of the Iles d'Hyères (7km by 3km) and easiest to reach, being only a 15-minute boat trip from la Tour Fondue (see Giens, page 68), Porquerolles' north coast has a series of sandy beaches and there are steep cliffs to the south. Boats land at the village of Ste-Agathe, facing the mainland, which has several hotels. Hiring a bicycle is probably the best way to cover the distance to the island's forts and other beaches; try Sun Bike Locations on boulevard de la Marine (tel: 94 57 39 11). Note: camping is prohibited, and so is smoking, outside the village. The islands often have a fresh water shortage, so bring your own mineral water with you.

If you don't want to stray far from the village, the 16th-century Fort Ste-Agathe has a good exhibition on underwater archaeology (open June to September). One of the most popular walks, or rides, is to take the lane south from the village to the Cap d'Arme and the lighthouse (open daily from 10am to noon and 2pm to 6pm). Allow 30 minutes on foot, 10 minutes by bicycle.

### *PORT-CROS*
#### *MAP REF: 113 D1*

Port-Cros is almost entirely forested. In the tiny village the National Park Acceuil (information centre) sells National Park publications and organises discovery walks.

Here, too, the landscape is dotted with fortresses, and the island is crisscrossed with paths which you must explore on foot. For more detailed descriptions of the walk suggested on page 73, see the National Park leaflets.

Plage de la Palud, to the west of the port, is particularly beautiful, and an 'underwater path' has been marked out from the shore to the Rocher du Rascas.

### *RAMATUELLE*
#### *MAP REF: 113 E2*

The St-Tropez peninsula produces some very drinkable wines, and one of the labels to look out for comes from Ramatuelle, a village at the heart of the peninsula which can trace its origins to the Saracen *Camatulli Corum*. Not surprisingly for a village only 11km from St-Tropez and with views towards the famous beaches of Pampelonne and Tahiti, many of the houses have been restored.

The steep road to the Plage de l'Escalet and also to the lighthouse at Cap Camaret are worth exploring. For the energetic, a long-distance coastal path runs from Cap Camaret south and west to the village of Gigaro, near the resort of La Croix-Valmer, facing across the Baie de Cavalaire to Cavalaire-sur-Mer.

**Nearby** A twisting, narrow road leads through the Col de Paillas and past the ruined Moulins de Paillas, to climb to another wine village, Gassin, originally known as *Gardia Sinus* and with superb views of the bays to the north and south of the peninsula.

### COUNTRY WALK

This walk or cycle ride combines some of Porquerolles' best beaches with a visit to a couple of its forts.

*Starting from the village, follow the coastal lane which leads below the fortress east from Ste-Agathe.*

After leaving the village, cycle for 15 to 20 minutes between the Plaine de la Courtade and the wooded shore of the Plage de la Courtade, before climbing towards the two forts on the headland. Perched on the Pointe du Lequin are the Fortin du Lequin, and the ruined L'Alycastre.

*Continue along the coastal path, descending towards the sea and the Plage Notre-Dame.*

The path ends at this long expanse of sand backed by trees, often deserted. Backtracking for a while, take the first left if you want to make the 15-minute ride to the fort on the Pointe du Galéasson; otherwise take the second left for the climb up towards the island's highest point, which is known as the Sémaphore.

*At the crossroads, turn left to reach the summit itself, right for the fort of La Repentance or straight on in order to rejoin the coastal path and return to the village.*

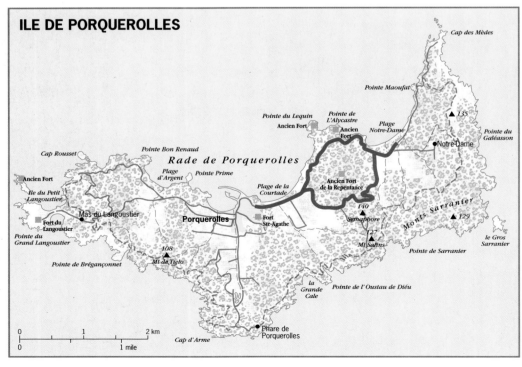

**ILE DE PORQUEROLLES**

# RIEZ

*MAP REF: 113 D3*

Many small towns of Provence were once bigger and more important than they are today, and Riez is no exception. Fifteen kilometres west of the smaller but more famous village of Moustiers-Ste-Marie (see page 70), Riez stands on the River Colostre on the edge of the Valensole plateau, a quiet agricultural town where the main local crop is lavender. In another field outside Riez stand four Roman columns (all that remains of a former temple) and slightly nearer town is preserved an early Christian baptistery which once stood next to the cathedral, itself long since abandoned.

In the town itself, many of the houses have fine Renaissance façades and have undergone recent restoration.

The original Roman village was above the present town on Mont St-Maxime, where a later chapel dedicated to the saint now stands, commanding an impressive view. **Nearby** The town of Valensole stands at the heart of its broad plateau, Provence's main lavender-growing area and, not surprisingly, a good centre for bee-keeping too. The Musée Vivant de l'Abeille on the Route de Manosque explains the science of apiculture as it used to be and is today (open weekdays and Saturday afternoons).

**The village of Ramatuelle, set on the St-Tropez peninsula**

ILE DE PORT-CROS

# COUNTRY WALK

*Start from the Fort du Moulin on Port-Cros.*

This is the oldest of the island's forts, with views across to Bagaud, another island. The windmill for which it is named was destroyed in the 19th century.

*Follow the botanical path lined with many Mediterranean species round the headland towards the Fort de l'Estissac.*

The fort was built in 1634 on Richelieu's orders.

*Take the path around the fort,*

*heading inland toward the Fort de l'Eminence.*

Built in 1875, this fort was used to hold German prisoners of war in 1914 and is now being restored. At a height of 138m, it commands an impressive view of the whole island.

*Continue south along the Route des Forts to a crossroads, where you turn right, and soon afterwards right again, to join the Vallon de la Solitude. Return to the port past the Manoir d'Hélène, or, for a longer walk, turn left towards La Vigie and the southern coast, returning along the Route des Crêtes and the Vallon de la Faussé-Monnaie.*

# ·*WILDLIFE*·

Provence has an abundance of wildlife, although this may not be obvious at first sight. The rough, scrubby countryside up in the hills, the *garrigue,* hides a variety of animals, notably wild boars, which will sometimes crash across your path when you wander off the beaten track. Comical in their appearance, the smaller family members are harmless, but the tusks of an aged adult rampaging male should be avoided! Wild boars are hunted in the season, but still somehow manage to survive, as do partridges and pheasants. Foxes abound; driving up through the pine forests you will often see them beside the road. You may also glimpse the beautiful and fearless pine martens which hunt for smaller prey like baby rabbits and have been known to scale the walls of houses in search of a place to hide with their food.

Above right: a glossy ibis
Below: thistle-down in the
Camargue

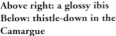

## NATURE PARKS

There are now many regional wildlife parks where you can leave your car and picnic, or enjoy tranquillity without meeting another human being, and have a chance of seeing these animals. One of the largest is the Lubéron Regional Nature Park, just east of Cavaillon in the direction of Manosque. Another, just north of Stes-Marie-de-la-Mer, is the Etang de Vaccarès, a regional nature park, which is host not only to birds but to wild horses, and in spring some wonderful wild flowers.

## PROVENCE'S BIRD LIFE

Provence is on the migratory route of many birds, flying from the warmth of Africa and the Near East to nesting places in the north. So if you are here in spring or autumn you could well be in for a bird spectacular. But you'll not be disappointed outside of the migration periods, for this region has a brilliant line-up of birds. In the upland and mountain areas you will be unlucky not to see the drifting shapes of eagles, while

smaller birds include gorgeous bee-eaters. And sometimes it seems that nightingales are singing from every bush (not just at night by any means).

The greatest concentration of birds, however, is to be found in the Camargue, notably around the *étangs,* or lagoons. Pink flamingos are a common sight here, and many wildfowl are to be seen. Gulls and cormorants are here in their hundreds. You will also see cattle egrets, which sit on the backs of grazing cattle catching the insects that plague them.

Despite European Community laws tens of thousands of birds are still shot in Provence every year by gunmen out to prove their machismo.

## VALLEYS AND MOUNTAINS

In winter the valleys are silent, but in summer the silence is broken by the bell-like call of tree frogs. Coloured vivid emerald green, they sound more like birds than amphibians, and can be heard during the day calling to one another beside streams. Then there is that typical Mediterranean sound, the clicking of cicadas, insects that are at their loudest in the midday sun.

Native snakes rustle through the grass, the largest of these – and the most frightening to look at – being the Montpellier snake *(couleuvre)*, which is totally harmless. The most deadly, however, is the asp. Instant medical treatment is needed if you are unlucky enough to be bitten by it, but it is seldom found at altitudes lower than 300m up, and the simple precaution of wearing trousers, socks and enclosed shoes when walking through the undergrowth should give protection. Small brown scorpions are common in Provence, hiding under stones or in damp corners in houses. Terrifying to look at, their bite is virtually harmless, at the worst similar to that of a wasp sting. The comical praying mantises are common, and so are fireflies and glow-worms in summer. The region also has a wealth of wonderful butterflies – the swallowtail, for instance.

To see just how rich the wildlife of the area is, visit the Harmas at Sérignan-du-Comtat, near Orange, a museum in the home of J H Fabre, a world-famous ento-mologist (1823–1915). He devoted his life to collecting insects, reptiles and small mammals, and wrote nearly a hundred books on the subject, which have been translated all over the world. Within the glass cabinets that cover the walls of his house is an extraordinary diversity of objects – shells, fossils, minerals, birds' nests with their eggs, and animal bones (and even some human ones found on the site of a cannibal tribe). There is a herbarium, too, showing local plants, mosses, lichens and fungi.

## FLORA

The wild flowers of Provence are legend and infinite in their variety. On the slopes of Mont Ventoux, above the snow line (which in summer can be picked out by the roadside posts that measure the depth of snow), you will find an extraordinary display of colourful alpine flowers. Here, high up on the mountains where the grass is short and stunted and parched in summer, you will find herds of grazing goats and the occasional sheep.

Clinging to the limestone outcrops on the mountains, somehow finding a foothold in the thin, badly nourished soil, grows a tapestry of plants that are basically survivors. These are the plants that

form the typical Provençal *garrigue:* herbs like thyme and oregano, lemon balm, bay and mint, stunted lavender and rosemary, which make the ground aromatic underfoot. Then there are spiny shrubs like the kermes oak, heathers, gorse and the pink-flowered cistus. Under their shelter there are wild flowers that add colour briefly in spring.

The umbrella pine with its spreading shape is a familiar sight in Provence. Forests of cedar grow on the slopes of the Petit Lubéron mountains, and in the Vivarais there are many chestnut trees, contributing to a regional industry for *marrons* (chestnuts) in the area.

## FOREST FIRES

A great danger in areas of woodland is forest fires, which cause destruction to both animal and, sometimes, human life. Montagne Ste-Victoire for instance, has been changed out of all recognition from the days of Cézanne by an enormous blaze

that reduced all its vegetation to a blackened scar. These forest fires are a constant threat. The problem is caused in part by the volatile oils of aromatic plants like rosemary, lavender and thyme which, mixed with dry, drought-ridden plants and pine needles, can catch light spontaneously during the summer months, flaring up like an incendiary bomb. However, many more fires are caused by careless picnickers. If the wind gets up, a Provençal fire can move with terrifying speed – as fast as 10km/h, devastating everything in its path. Prompt action by the fire brigade helps to limit the damage, but sometimes it is necessary to 'bomb' the blaze with water: slow, lumbering Canadair planes based at Marseille's airport scoop up water from the sea, dropping their 'catch' on the forests below.

**The praying mantis is a common sight in Provence**

## ROQUEBRUNE-SUR-ARGENS

*MAP REF: 113 E2*

As its name suggests, the village lies beneath a mighty, deep-red rock, the Montagne de Roquebrune (372m), which dominates the Argens valley 12km west of Fréjus. The church and arcaded houses date from the 16th century, although the site is much older, and the tall stone clock tower with a collection of sundials and wrought-iron belfry is typical of the Var.

Apart from an excursion to the summit of Roquebrune itself, there are also good views to be had from two nearby chapels: Notre-Dame-de-la-Roquette, to the west of the mountain, and above the village, Notre-Dame-de-la-Pitié.

76

## ST-RAPHAEL

*MAP REF: 113 E2*

The uncharitable might say that St-Raphaël is one of those South of France resorts that have basked in the glamour of the Côte d'Azur without really deserving to. Despite its Grand Casino and new pleasure port, it is in fact an unpretentious place, with a sandy beach and shops full of beach toys rather than *couture* bikinis – ideal for families. In summer, the best time to visit is during the International Jazz Festival (usually the first week in July) when bands give impromptu performances throughout town all day, and in the evening the promenade de

**St-Raphaël, a cheerful South of France resort which is ideal for family holidays**

Lattre de Tassigny becomes an open-air theatre with people perching on plant pots to listen to the free late-night concerts. The quai Albert-1er and cours Jean Bart around the harbour are strung with lights, and craft stalls stay open until the early hours.

Unless you have already visited Fréjus to the west, you might be surprised to learn that St-Raphaël has been welcoming 'visitors' since the Romans. To see a different side of the town, head inland and take the rue Basso under the railway bridge, following rue Gambetta (past several good *boulangeries* selling the local speciality, *pan bagnat*) and bear left at place Carnot to reach the tiny old quarter of town.

In the rue des Templiers the bar of the Hôtel Les Templiers is a popular local haunt and a good

**Roquebrune-sur-Argens has 16th-century buildings set on an ancient site**

place to enjoy a slow *pastis* after a visit to the market opposite. Also across from the hotel is the Romanesque Templars' church with its wrought-iron belfry, illuminated at night, atop a tower originally built for defence from seaborne invaders. In the tiny square beyond is a small archaeological museum.

**For history buffs** St-Raphaël's early history can be charted by objects that have been retrieved from the sea. At the Musée d'Archéologie Sous-Marine in the place de la Vieille-Eglise, Roman amphorae are displayed alongside presentations of the underwater archaeological techniques used to retrieve them.

# MOTOR TOUR

St-Raphaël stands at the western end of the Massif de l'Esterel – a dramatic series of peaks of dark red volcanic rock which drop down to the sea along the Corniche de l'Esterel. The circuit as far as La Napoule and back is 50km.

*From the church in the old town follow the avenue Général de Gaulle (D98c) towards Fréjus, turning right to join the N7, which mostly follows the route of the Roman Via Aurelia around the northern side of the Esterel.*

### Notre-Dame de Jerusalem
Shortly after the junction with the D37 the road passes a Buddhist pagoda on the right-hand side, its single chamber brightly decorated with murals (there is a mosque near by on the D4 north from Fréjus). Five kilometres further, a turning to the right leads to the Notre-Dame-de-Jérusalem, a chapel decorated by Jean Cocteau. The road is twisty and wooded, but there are occasional views across to the west.

*After about 11km a turning on the right leads towards the summit of Mont Vinaigre (618m), the highest of the Esterel peaks. Turn left next to the forester's lodge and left again at the junction before the Col de l'Aire de l'Olivier.*

### Col de l'Aire de l'Olivier
On a clear day, the walk to the summit is rewarded with a full

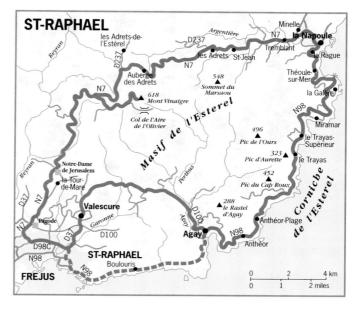

panorama along the coast and inland to the Alps.

*Return to the N7 and continue past the Auberge des Adrets, haunt of a notorious 18th-century highwayman, Gaspard de Besse, who once terrorised travellers on this lonely stretch of road. Continue towards Mandelieu and Cannes, but turn right to La Napoule before the bridge under the autoroute.*

### La Napoule
This small resort makes a dramatic start to the Corniche drive, with the seafront dominated by an imposing castle. The original 14th-century building was much altered by the American sculptor Henry Clews, whose works you can see by taking an afternoon guided tour. The small gardens and

exterior of the castle, fascinating in themselves, are free to visit.

*The Corniche (N98) now begins to wind westwards past a succession of small bays and resorts. The red rock, green trees and blue sea appear in dramatic combinations, but be careful where you park if you stop to admire the view.*

### Théoule-sur-Mer
The port of La Rague is followed by the pleasant resort of Théoule-sur-Mer, with a small 'château' of its own and the first of many excellent viewpoints, the Pointe de l'Aiguille. Past the Pointe de l'Esquillon, where you can drive up to another viewpoint, Miramar is a busy, built-up resort on the deep bay of La Figueirette, while Le Trayas offers a series of attractive rocky coves which you can explore.

Anthéor-Plage and Anthéor lie below the peaks of Cap Roux, before Agay, whose deep, curved harbour makes it one of the most popular along the Corniche de l'Esterel – and one of the oldest, having been used since at least Roman times. Its beaches are overlooked from the northeast by the red cliffs of Le Rastel d'Agay peak (288m) and this is the best point to turn inland to explore the Massif de l'Esterel itself: branch right again after 2km for the twisting climb to the Pic d'Aurelle (323m) and the Pic d'Ours (496m).

*Return to St-Raphaël either along the coast, via Boulouris, or inland via the village of Valescure.*

**The red volcanic rock of the Massif de l'Esterel, near St-Raphaël**

## ST-TROPEZ

*MAP REF: 113 E1*

The reason for St-Tropez's reputed exclusivity becomes apparent when you make the trip by car at the height of summer – it can still be difficult to get into. A more civilised and appropriate approach – given its history of seaborne invasion and the days when it had to rely on fishing for a living – is by boat from Ste-Maxime or St-Raphaël.

The first thing you notice (and it can be quite a shock if you are expecting a second Cannes) is how small St-Tropez is, hardly any bigger than the fishing village that inspired the neo-impressionist and Fauvist painters at the turn of the century and attracted the film directors and stars, led by Vadim and Bardot, in the 1960s.

It is also very pretty, despite the often vulgar conspicuous wealth. A few feet from the red canopies of the expensive cafés that line the quai de Suffren – front stalls for enjoying the spectacle – vast white yachts dwarf the tiny port, decks groaning with whole dining suites, silverware and *objets d'art*. If you prefer to view all this from a distance, there are several alternatives: walk out to the end of the Môle Jean-Réveille, climb to the citadel which overlooks the

town or make the longer excursion to the chapel of Ste-Anne, via avenue Roussel.

Another good but less well-known view is from the tiny balcony outside the first-floor window of the Musée de l'Annonciade, at the southwest corner of the harbour. This exceptional collection of modern art includes works by Signac, Dufy, Matisse and Bonnard, often of St-Tropez itself, supplemented with high-quality exhibitions. The town – and its tourists – still attract artists today whose work can be seen on the quayside outside the museum.

Beyond quai Jean-Jaurès to the east of the harbour, the picturesque streets of the quartier de la Ponche lead past the Hôtel de Ville and baroque church to the tiny and remarkably quiet Port de Pêche. Rue de la Citadelle takes the most direct route up to the Renaissance fortifications, which house a maritime and local history museum. Contemporary culture – of the commercial kind – is on display in St-Tropez's more exclusive shops in the streets to the west of the port.

From rue du Général Allard, alleys lead to the place des Lices, the twice-weekly market place, and one of St-Tropez's most painted places, the Café des Arts.

**Nearby** The other famous names associated with St-Tropez are its beaches, though all but the plage des Graniers lie a few kilometres away around the headland, including the plages des Salins, de Tahiti and de Pampelonne. Inland from the Cap de St-Tropez, near the plage de Salins, the Château de la Moutte is open to visitors. A coastal path follows the peninsula from the plage des Graniers via the Cap de St-Tropez to the Cap du Pinet, near Tahiti beach.

### THE LEGEND OF ST-TROPEZ

According to tradition, a Roman centurion named Torpes was beheaded and his body set adrift in a boat, watched over by a faithful dog and a cockerel. The boat landed here on the peninsula, and the village was named after him. The origins of nearby Cogolin are similarly explained and named after the cock. In May one of St-Tropez's two *bravades* takes place – a procession 'of defiance' through the streets parading the statue of St-Tropez.

**Fishing village turned fashionable resort: St-Tropez**

Crowds invade the sandy beaches of Ste-Maxime, on the Golfe de St-Tropez

towards Cap Sicié. A right turn towards the cliffs and a steep climb brings you to the chapel of Notre-Dame-du-Mai with its small museum of ex-votos and panoramic views. For those who enjoy exhilarating cliff walks, a path leads from the chapel west to the hamlet of La Leque.

## SISTERON
### MAP REF: 113 D3

Approaching Provence from Dauphiné, Sisteron leaves you in no doubt that here you are entering another *pays*. It has long guarded the pass in the mountains of Haute-Provence through which the Durance squeezes, joined more recently by the tunnelling N85 and A51 autoroute, from which you get your first views of the imposing fortifications of the citadel.

The citadel dates from the 12th century, later extended by Jean Erard and then Vauban as a link in the *corset des forteresses* against Savoy (see Colmars/Entrevaux on pages 66 and 67). The Corps de Garde houses the Musée de la Citadelle (open daily mid-March to mid-September), explaining the history of the fortress and its occupants through paintings and documents. Energetic children can let off steam running around the ramparts; adults can catch their breath further up in the Guérite du Diable watch-tower.

**Sisteron, with its citadel looming over the Durance**

## STE-MAXIME
### MAP REF: 113 E2

Ste-Maxime is where Bandol wants to be. Less than 4km across the Golfe de St-Tropez from its famous neighbour, it has the required casino, palm trees and large marina which spell serious South of France spending – but it still has the air of a family resort.

If watersports and sandy beaches are not enough, take the D25 (Route du Muy) into the Massif des Maures and follow the River Couloubrier for 10km to the Domaine de St-Donat. The Musée de la Musique Méchanique et du Phonographe is a fascinating private collection charting the evolution of the phonograph from Edison to quadraphonics, along with magic lanterns, music boxes and the early days of cinema and television.

In Ste-Maxime itself, the Musée des Traditions Locales in place Alziers illustrates the geology, history and customs of the Golfe de St-Tropez with models and film.

## SANARY-SUR-MER
### MAP REF: 113 D1

Sanary lies in the shadow of neighbouring Bandol, and insists that it, too, is on the Côte d'Azur, although it lies at the western end of an urban stretch that crosses the peninsula of Cap Sicié via Six-Fours-les-Plages to Toulon. Follow the D616 coast road instead and you come to the small port of Le Brusc, from where ferries make

the 12-minute trip to another of the Ricard islands (see page 62), the Ile des Embiez.

Much larger than its neighbour, Bendor, Embiez also has plenty of opportunity for water sports, but with its ruined château and varied scenery there is far more here for the visitor in search of a few hours away from it all. The main attraction is the Nouvel Espace Muséal et Aquarium, a scientific and educational complex with some fascinating aquatic inmates (open daily except Wednesday mornings out of season).

Back on the mainland, the road continues around the headland

The pottery produced at Moustiers has gained worldwide recognition

# PROVENCE'S ECONOMY

**Provence's economy is an intriguing mix of old and new, with traditional crops thriving alongside high-tech industries. This infusion of new life into what had been largely an argricultural system can be seen in the growing number of signs pointing to the *zone industrielle* on the outskirts of major towns.**

The South, with its friendly climate, has become host in the last few years to many new enterprises, from electronics to confectionary and clothing. The most popular site is the valley of the Rhône, with its first-class communication network. In addition to the airports at Avignon and Marseille, the region is well served by road by the Autoroute du Sud from Paris and the North, while the Train à Grand Vitesse (TGV) which achieves speeds of over 250km/h, goes from Paris to Avignon in just over four and a half hours. There are plans to extend it to Nice, which will cut the current journey time of seven hours.

## TRADITIONAL INDUSTRIES
Many of the old industries still hold their own – the perfume industry at Grasse on the Riviera, for instance, surrounded by fields of flowers, and the making of crystallised fruits in the Apt area. There are also oils and soaps made from local lavender and olives. Bauxite, used in the making of aluminium, is still mined at Brignoles and Les Baux, and there are salt beds at Hyères and in the Camargue, where the trade dates back to the monks in the 13th century. France's largest wine producer, Listel, is also located in the Camargue. Old trades like the mining of pigments from the ochre quarries at Roussillon in the

Vaucluse and on the slopes of Mont Ventoux are still worked, though on a lesser scale, as are the cork oak forests of the Maures.

## THE TEXTILE INDUSTRY
Another traditional trade that has been revived is in the realm of fashion.

Provence has always been involved in textiles, from the days when many of the hill villagers raised silkworms for the weavers of Lyon. The world-famous fabric denim came originally from Nîmes, and was made up into workwear for farmers and fishermen. Traditional Provençal prints in patterns that go back several hundred years are now making a comeback in both fashion and furnishing fabrics, with big chains like Habitat and Laura Ashley featuring them in their collections.

These prints are derived from *les Indiennes*, patterned fabrics from India which were landed in Marseille in the 1600s and quickly became a fashion, with the French court as well as ordinary people. This so severely affected the French textile industry that their import was eventually banned. It was then that the Provençal fabric houses thought up the idea of copying and adapting the designs for themselves, and so 'Provençal' prints were born.

Largely responsible for the current revival is the house of

Souleiado, based in Tarascon. In 1938, Charles Demery, its managing director, took over an almost defunct family firm dating from the 17th century, and breathed new life into it. With more than 40,000 original fruitwood blocks of the traditional prints to draw on, Souleiado now has shops all over the world and, apart from selling furnishing and dress fabrics, also markets tiles, wallpaper and other items. Souleiado's intriguing museum at Tarascon is open most days and is well worth a visit. Not far away is the rival house Les Olivades, also in the throes of opening shops abroad.

## NEW INDUSTRY

The modern face of Provence can be seen in the new town of Sophia-Antipolis, near Antibes (see page 88). Here, the community is based around high-tech, scientific and communications industries, which may well represent the Riviera's future development.

## FARMING

Despite all the excitement on the industrial front, farming still plays a vital role in the economy of Provence. *Les primeurs*, early crops of fruit and vegetables – notably asparagus, strawberries, peaches, cherries and melons – are grown in and around the valley of the River Durance, with its fertile soil, and on the Vaucluse plateau. The picturesque fields of sunflowers that Van Gogh loved to paint yield valuable cooking oil.

Provençal olives and olive oil are famous all over the world, though the industry suffered a blow when, some 25 years ago, a punishing late frost killed off many of the trees in the Vaucluse. Only the areas around Salon-de-Provence and Nyons survived. Olive trees have been replaced over recent years with cherry trees, which now provide bumper crops of fruit. Ironically, as the olive industry dwindles in some areas, there is a brisk trade in *scourtins*, the round fibre mats on which the fruit is traditionally pressed. They are bought by tourists to use as place mats on the dinner table, and a visit to a *moulin à l'huile* goes on many an itinerary.

## LAVENDER, HONEY AND HERBS

More than 8,000 hectares of lavender are grown in Provence, especially in the Vaucluse, on the slopes of mountain ranges. Two varieties are used: the aromatic version that most of us know, and *lavandin*, which is less fragrant but produces more oil per plant.

Both types are distilled within two or three days of picking, then used in the perfume and soap industry. A museum of lavender has recently opened at Coustellet, near Gordes, in the Lubéron, and is well worth a visit.

Honey is another thriving small industry and *miel au lavande*, with its pungent, perfumed taste is another regional speciality for tourists to take home. Almonds are still grown in the south, mainly to be made into sugared *calissons*, manufactured in the Salon area.

Herbs, too, provide a good livelihood for small entrepreneurs and smallholders. They are grown mainly for flavourings and *tisanes* (herb teas). The lime flower *(tilleul)* is popular for teas, and now there are orchards of lime trees to be seen in the region around Mont Ventoux, especially Carpentras. Herbes de Provence – a mix of many herbs, notably thyme and savory, that are gathered in the wild – have become a popular flavouring the world over; and there are specialist growers of tarragon and marjoram in the Vaucluse.

## PROVENCE'S LIVESTOCK

Apart from goats and sheep up in the mountains and a few merino sheep in the Bouches-du-Rhône area, there is relatively little livestock in Provence. The one exception is the Camargue, which prides itself on raising two types of animal: magnificent black bulls which frequently star at Provençal bull-fights, and white horses, which are allowed to run wild and are herded from time to time by the *gardians*, the cowboys.

Another traditional industry that still survives is fishing, with Marseille being the main port for landing the catch. Because of pollution in the Mediterranean, few large fish are now caught, and much of the fish on display in the Provençal markets comes from Brittany and other northern ports.

## TOURISM

Tourism is a staple part of Provence's economy. More and more foreigners are buying holiday or retirement homes here, and restaurants and hotels are benefiting from a new type of trade: business conferences, particularly popular on the coast. Held, as they are, off-season, conferences are reviving the older fashion for holidaying in winter on the Riviera and bringing in custom all year round.

**Gigondas produces a powerful red Provençal wine (see page 51)**

# •TOULON•

82

Toulon, France's second-largest naval base, is a surprisingly lively and likeable place, certainly a working city, not a leisured one, and a good touring base for exploring the lesser-known *départements* of Var and Alpes-de-Haute-Provence. The city centre lies at the heart of a vast natural harbour, or *rade*, backed by limestone hills and protected from the sea by the peninsula of St-Mandrier, one of several suburbs that make up the city. The nearest beaches are around the headland at Le Mourillon and across the harbour at Les Sablettes, as Toulon's main 'seafront' was completely destroyed in World War II and is now a rather sad marina lined with cafés.

Getting your bearings is straightforward. Behind the harbour, the maze that is old Toulon (map ref: 113 D1) has survived intact; the main core is pedestrianised and lively during the day, less welcoming at night, although some of the more run-down central quarters are undergoing renovation. North of the old town, Toulon's main thoroughfare is a boulevard worthy of central Paris – at least for the speed of the traffic, which is not surprising, since at either end it continues as the A50 autoroute. On the north side is place de la Liberté, a spacious square with carousel, fountain and telephone kiosks, and a grid of broad, 19th-century streets.

## GETTING AROUND

Like many cities, Toulon is not much fun to drive around, especially when it has such an efficient public transport system, which extends to its neighbouring suburbs and includes the novelty of boats as well as buses. A one-day *Carte Cigale* allows unlimited travel on all RMTT services and could include, for instance, a boat trip to La Seyne-sur-Mer, bus to the beaches at Les Sablettes or St-Mandrier and return boat trip to Toulon. Boats leave regularly from the *embarcadère* on quai Stalingrad, where you can also buy single tickets.

**The 11th-century Cathédrale Ste-Marie in Toulon**

## MONT FARON AND THE SUBURBS

Toulon's strategic importance is apparent from a ring of forts, both along the coast and in the hills, and one of the best ways to see the whole of the city is to climb to one of the highest, at the summit of Mont Faron. The Tour Beaumont has become a museum devoted to the Débarquement, the liberation of southeast France by Allied forces in 1944, with a memorial to the soldiers who took part in the action, a diaorama, an exhibition of photographs, weapons and uniforms of the time, and a film of the landings. Outside, the views from the terrace give a complete panorama of the city, the harbour and Mont Caume to the north.

The approach by car is exhilarating: the route du Faron is one-way and should be approached from the west, passing the memorial and the zoo before dropping down again to join the Corniche Marius Escartefigue, with more views. An alternative is to take the *téléphérique* (cable car), which runs from the terminus on boulevard Amiral Vence.

From the coast at Le Mourillon, you can follow a scenic footpath called the Sentier des Douaniers around Cap Brun and its fort. Another of the forts around Toulon, the oldest and open to visitors, is the Tour Royale, named for Louis XII. This guards the *Petite Rade*, or inner harbour, at pointe de la Mitre. From the roof terrace you can see Fort de Balaguier across the harbour, built by Richelieu to attack the Tour Royale opposite, and now another Musée Naval.

The peninsula is well-worth exploring by car. The D18 follows the north-facing coast with superb views stretching across to the mainland, past the town of La Seyne, the two forts and the scenic Corniche de Tamaris and between the stilted fishing cabins and beach at Les Sablettes to St-Mandrier.

**Nearby** In the valley between Mont Faron and Mont Caume, the village of Le-Revest-les-Eaux is a peaceful antidote to the tower blocks and cranes of Toulon, with a 17th-century château, the ancient Tree of Liberty in front of the church, Saracen tower and smaller lookout tower, le Saraillon, on the road to the barrage.

There are several interesting walks near by, all of which are marked with arrows – ask at the tourist office for full details.

# TOWN WALK

Central Toulon is compact enough to visit its main sights in a day. Allow enough time to visit any or all of the museums *en route*.

*Start from place de la Liberté.*

1 You can detour a short distance along avenue Général-Léclerc to two of Toulon's main museums, the Musée d'Histoire Naturelle and the Musée de Toulon (the city's principal art gallery) with particularly fine modern and contemporary collections – both housed in the same building next to the Jardin Alexandre-1er.

*From place de la Liberté cross the boulevard and continue down rue Pastoureau. Turn left into rue Jean-Jaurès which leads to place Victor-Hugo and the front of the Théâtre.*

2 This popular meeting place marks the start of the pedestrianised streets, which you can follow all the way to the harbour. Continue straight ahead for the smaller place des Trois Dauphins, named for the mossy fountain that does indeed feature three 18th-century dolphins as well as a variety of vegetation.

*Bear right in the square and follow rue Hoche and rue d'Alger. Branch off left and right to discover the many atmospheric streets of the old town.*

3 Before you reach the water ahead, you must negotiate the busy avenue de la République. To make a detour here to the city's other main museum, turn right and continue to place Ingénieur Général de Monsenergue (on the corner). Opposite you will see the gates to the Arsenal, floodlit at night, and the Musée Naval, an impressive collection of the art and science associated with ships and their sailors through history to the present.

*Walk along the quai Stalingrad past the embarking point for the RMTT ferries and the boats to Porquerolles and Port-Cros (see page 72).*

4 The former town hall, with its doorway held up by Puget's pair of mighty *Atlantes*, stands out as the only seemingly ancient building on the quayside. In fact, the statues representing *Fatigue* and *Force* were put here after safekeeping during World War II, and the building now houses municipal offices and occasional exhibitions in the ground floor hall. The quai is lined with cafés and, though not conventionally picturesque, the view across the calm, shimmering water with the marina to the left is quite mesmerising.

*Turning away from the water and recrossing the avenue opposite the baroque St-François church you arrive in place Louis-Blanc, at the southern end of the cours Lafayette.*

5 Halfway up on the left, the traverse de la Cathédrale leads to the classical façade and vast bell tower of the Cathédrale Ste-Marie, although the building behind dates

**Toulon's quai Stalingrad**

from the 11th century, with more works by Puget and his pupils. Returning to the cours, the Musée du Vieux Toulon is near by. Opposite the museum, detour down rue Garibaldi, where in place Armand Vallée the Porte d'Italie is a surviving example of the city's gates in the 18th century and now site of a thriving café-theatre. Return to the cours along rue Courdouan.

*At the top of the cours, rue Paul Landrin returns, left, to place des Trois Dauphins, from where rue Molière leads alongside the Théâtre to the boulevard de Strasbourg.*

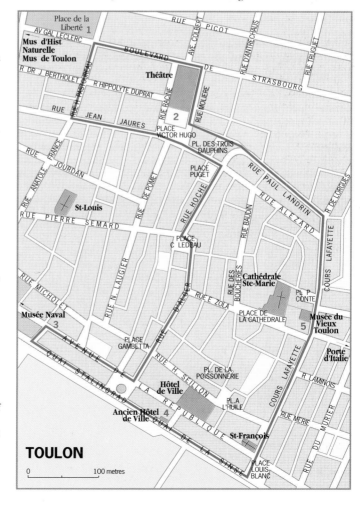

TOULON

0          100 metres

# ALPES-MARITIMES & COTE D'AZUR

The southeast corner of Provence is the land of both F Scott Fitzgerald's *Tender Is the Night* and Graham Greene's *J'Accuse*. The Riviera of the 1920s has certainly changed, embracing business conference centres and high-tech industries as easily as the discreet villas of its wealthier visitors, but there is still a certain glitter at the Cannes Film Festival or at Monaco which, together with the climate, continue to attract the glamorous and the curious alike. The coast does not have a monopoly on the theatrical, however: inland, the *département* of Alpes-Maritimes makes a dramatic backdrop, with almost inaccessible hilltop villages and some of the country's most popular ski resorts only a short, often breathtaking, drive away.

On the Côte itself, with its three corniches (coastal roads) between Nice and Cap-Martin, driving can be a pleasure, but the main towns are also well connected by fast and frequent train and bus services. Nice is the southern terminus for the Chemin de Fer de Provence, a narrow-gauge railway which rattles into the mountains and on to Digne via historic villages such as Entrevaux and Annot (see Var and Alpes-de-Haute-Provence). Motorists who prefer to escape the heat and crowds along the coast will find even more challenging driving inland, on tortuous, twisting roads which hug the wooded peaks and tunnel into steep, rocky gorges.

The *département* of Alpes-Maritimes is roughly the shape of a maple leaf, with its veins a network of river valleys flowing to the sea. The most northerly point encompasses the Tinée valley and the remote Parc National du Mercantour, where you can try to spot chamois, mouflon and the rare ibex; here also are the ski resorts of Isola 2000 and Auron. To the west lie the valleys of the Var and the Esteron, with the dramatic dark red gorges of Cians and Daluis and the narrower, deep clefts called *clues*. East lie the more mountainous Vésubie, with its alpine lakes and forests, and the historic Roya, with its ancient towns of Sospel, Breil and Tende and distinctive architecture. The hills behind the coast, known as the Haute Pays, can also be divided into the distinct regions around Grasse, Vence, Nice and Menton.

The *département*'s eastern boundary with neighbouring Italy is a relatively new one: Nice, as part of the Duchy of Savoy, only became part of France in 1860 and the Italian influence is still strong in the Roya valley. Menton was added the following year, bought from the Grimaldis of Monaco. It is easy to forget that the region has a history far longer than that of the Riviera, but all along the coast you can find evidence of the Roman era, most impressive perhaps at La Turbie, while west of Tende the Vallée des Merveilles and the Vallon de Fontanalbe preserve stone carvings from the Bronze Age.

As well as discovering the more unusual attractions of this area – from scaling frozen cascades in winter to searching out exquisite

**Top: Levens, a medieval town which sits near the Vésubie and Var valleys**
**Left: a beach view at Cannes**

church organs in the Roya valley –
it is also worth remembering the
differences between the coastal
resorts themselves, equally famous
perhaps but all very different in
character. Nice is a large city,
vibrant and sometimes hustling;
Cannes has its more conspicuous
wealth arranged neatly around a
long, curving bay parcelled up by
the big hotels; Menton is quieter,
with a beautiful old quarter, a

sandy beach and turquoise water;
Antibes has an ancient castle, but
the beaches on the Cap are mainly
private. In between lie smaller
resorts: Villefranche, Beaulieu-sur-
Mer and the Iles de Lérins, all with
attractions of their own. For a
bird's-eye view of the coast, do not
forget that Alpes-Maritimes has the
most famous – and most crowded
– *villages perchés* in the region.
However, there is plenty more to

**The tiny but glamorous
principality of Monaco crowding
on to its rocky headland**

discover – including Ste-Agnes
above Menton, which is thought
to be Europe's highest perched
village, at 754m – as well as the
smart galleries and fashion
boutiques of Eze and St-Paul-de-
Vence.

Genuine masterpieces can be
found throughout the region, with
modern art particularly well-
represented. You can see works
by Chagall and Matisse at Nice,
Picasso at Antibes and Vallauris,
Cocteau at Menton and
Villefranche, as well as one of the
greatest collections in the world at
the Fondation Maeght, St-Paul-de-
Vence.

For a region which appeals so
much to the senses, it is
appropriate that Alpes-Maritimes
also has some of the greatest
names in restaurants: those built
on the reputation of the chef such
as Roger Vergé's Le Moulin de
Mougins and celebrated dining
rooms of the great hotels, such as
the Négresco's Chantecler at Nice,
La Réserve at Beaulieu and the
Louis XV at Monte Carlo's Hôtel de
Paris.

Of course, you can also eat very
well in the Alpes-Maritimes
without breaking the bank –
whether you search out authentic
Niçois dishes in Vieux Nice or a
traditional hearty feast in an Alpine
*auberge*.

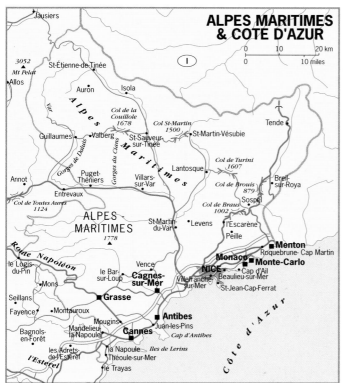

**ALPES MARITIMES
& COTE D'AZUR**

0          10          20 km
0                    10 miles

A statue in Nice of Queen Victoria,
once a visitor

# ·*THE RIVIERA*·

Technically speaking, the French Riviera starts at St-Raphaël and
ends at Menton on the Italian border, with Monaco accounting for
a small segment of coastline. Cannes and Nice, the twin capitals of
the Côte d'Azur, as this coastal strip is also called, have very
different personalities. Cannes seems the newer and brasher of the
two, more of a tourist resort, while dignified Nice (Edward Lear
described it as Belgravia) has retained much of its original
Provençal character. In addition to the two main resorts, the strip
encompasses fashionable places like Juan-les-Pins and Antibes,
Villefranche, Beaulieu, and St-Jean-Cap-Ferrat, where Somerset
Maugham lived. Inland, beyond the corniches, or coastal roads,
there are beautiful hill villages like Vence, Eze and La Turbie.
St-Tropez, which is often mistakenly called a Riviera resort, is
45km to the southwest.

## BEGINNINGS

The British author Tobias Smollett
is credited with being the first
person to use the Riviera as a
resort when he came to Nice in
the 1760s (when it was still under
Italian rule), hoping to cure
himself of consumption, as
tuberculosis was then called. His
mention of the area in his book
*Travels Through France and Italy*
inspired a number of his readers to
settle in the area. In no time at all
an English colony established itself
at Nice, and the newcomers built
the promenade des Anglais along
the seafront in the 1820s – the
scene, many years later, of the
death of dancer Isadora Duncan in
a freak accident.

## OPENING UP

In 1834 Lord Brougham, then
Britain's Lord Chancellor, decided
to take his daughter Eleonore to
the Mediterranean to recuperate
from an illness. Heading for Italy,
he found himself marooned in a
tiny fishing village called Cannes,
unable to cross the frontier
because of a cholera epidemic in
Nice. He found the place so much
to his liking that he bought some
land and made plans to build a
house, to take advantage of the
mild winters. Lord Brougham
returned to Cannes every winter
for 30 years, and in doing so
popularised it with his fellow
countrymen. One of the first
people to join him was millionaire
Sir Thomas Robinson Woodfield,
who built an estate of villas for
other would-be residents.

In 1860 Nice voted to become
part of France, and the following
year Menton, owned by the Prince
of Monaco, was sold to the French

for 4 million francs. At that time the roads were treacherous and uneven, but when the railroad was completed along the coast in 1864 it opened up the Riviera to visitors.

## A FASHIONABLE RESORT

It was during the 1860s that the Riviera became the most fashionable destination in Europe. Among the crowned heads that visited Nice – by then a burgeoning town – was Queen Victoria. The Tsar of Russia, together with the Russian court, made the Riviera their second home, which explains why Russian churches, with their characteristic onion domes, can be found in both Nice and Cannes. The ailing Tsarevitch Nicolas was brought to Nice in the hope of a cure, but he died there of consumption in 1865. Many people, in fact, came to the South of France believing that the climate was good for such illnesses. Some – Robert Louis Stevenson among them – did recover, but the numerous foreign cemeteries, segregated by nationality, tell a different tale. Most people however, came for the fun – the first casinos were opened in 1907, at a time when gambling was banned in many other places in Europe.

World War I saw a temporary eclipse in the fortunes of the Côte d'Azur. Places like Nice's Négresco Hotel, built during the Belle Epoque, became a military hospital and was left in a badly damaged condition. After hostilities had ended, in the 1920s, the Russian and German aristocracies were conspicuous by their absence, but a new type of visitor took their place.

Rich Americans arrived in droves, as did many of the brightest stars of stage and opera. And there to chronicle their activities was F Scott Fitzgerald and his wife Zelda. The season lengthened, sunbathing became the fashion, and the main influx of visitors switched from winter to summer. It is said that what triggered this reversal was an impromptu Fourth of July party given by the wealthy American Benjamin Finney at Antibes' Hôtel du Cap in 1926. Among the 70 or more guests were Ernest Hemingway, Noel Coward and, of course, the Fitzgeralds. Composer Cole Porter stayed at Antibes when it was still a virtually unknown headland; his friends, wealthy Bostonians Gerald and Sara Murphy, bought a house there, just below the lighthouse,

and entertained guests such as Gertrude Stein and Picasso. Fitzgerald immortalised the Murphys as Dick and Nicole Diver in his book *Tender is the Night*. A villa at Menton was bought by writer Katherine Mansfield, and today a street is named after her in the residential suburb of Garavan.

Royalty did not desert the coast, however. The Prince of Wales, later to abdicate from the British throne, arrived on his private yacht, and King Faisal of Saudi Arabia and Emperor Bao Dai of Vietnam were part of an exotic list that also included the wealthy Aga Khan. And a lady by the name of Wallis Simpson came to the Riviera during this time to stay at the Hôtel Provençal owned by millionaire Frank Gould.

## CANNES

Film stars, too, began to put in an appearance: Charlie Chaplin, for instance, Douglas Fairbanks and Maurice Chevalier, prefigured the annual gathering of stars at the Cannes Film Festival. The first festival was held in 1939 just before the outbreak of World War II, and it was here, at the Palais des Festivals et des Congrès, in 1955, that Prince Rainier of Monaco met and fell in love with Grace Kelly.

## THE STARS RETURN

In World War II, the Riviera, as part of General Pétain's uneasy truce, at first escaped enemy occupation. Then in November 1942 the Italians marched in. American troops liberated the area in August 1944, but in doing so they wrecked a large number of famous buildings. It took several years to restore the coast to its former glory. But it wasn't long before the celebrities returned, Errol Flynn and Gary Cooper among them. Cary Grant came, too, and wrote to a friend that the service in his hotel was so luxurious that they 'even ironed the laces of my tennis shoes'. Picasso set up a studio in Antibes. In the years that followed, other places along the coast came under the spotlight, notably a fishing village called St-Tropez, which shot to fame when Roger Vadim filmed Brigitte Bardot there.

Through it all the Riviera has managed to hold its own as the world capital of chic. The French themselves have discovered it, and these days, in July and August, it is crammed with a fascinating mix of very rich and ordinary holiday makers all taking advantage of the sun, with campsites at one end of the tourist scale and gigantic luxury hotels at the other.

The Cannes Film Festival celebrated in sculpture

## ANTIBES

MAP REF: 113 E2

Guarding the eastern shoulder of
the exclusive Cap d'Antibes, this
bustling town once also marked
the southeastern boundary of
France, where it squared up to
Nice (then part of the Duchy of
Savoy) across the Baie des Anges.
The American glitterati of the
1920s might have claimed to have
'discovered' the Cap, but Antibes
itself was first settled by Greek
traders in the 4th century BC. It has
a delightful old quarter, still
centred on its château and market,
which seems a world away from
the resorts all around.

For those arriving by train, or by
road from the east, the ramparts of
Vauban's Fort Carré are a
distinctive landmark on the edge
of the large marina. To reach the
old quarter direct, rather than via
the grid of streets around place
Général de Gaulle, enter the town
at the Porte Marine (sea gate) next
to the Port Vauban, and follow the
avenue de Amiral-de-Grasse along
the old sea ramparts to the
château. Once owned by the
Grimaldi family and still named for
them, the castle today is an ideal
backdrop to the Musée Picasso, a
collection which centres on the
paintings and sculptures produced
here by the artist when he used it
as his studio in 1946, together

with work by artists such as
Nicolas de Staël, Léger and Ernst
(closed Tuesdays, national holidays
and November; admission charge).
Across the tiny place du Château
stands the elegant and crumbling
Cathedral of the Immaculate
Conception and, below, the Hôtel
de Ville and the long cours
Masséna. The cours is best-known
for its Provençal food market
(daily except Mondays), but you
will also find a craft and *brocante*
market on Tuesday and Friday
afternoons. There is another
antiques and second-hand market
on place Audiberti on Thursdays,
while serious buyers might
consider the two-week antiques
fair in early April.

Antibes is known as the 'rose
capital' of France and is home of
the world-famous Roseraies
Meilland. Horticulturalists can also
visit the 19th-century arboretum at
the Villa Thuret on Cap d'Antibes,
and a new Mediterranean botanic
attraction known as Exflora, a 5-
hectare park at Antibes-les-Pins.

To discover more about the early
years of Antibes and the people
who lived here, continue along
the avenue de Amiral-de-Grasse to
the archaeological museum in the
St-André Bastion (closed Tuesdays
in winter and all November;
admission charge).
**Nearby** In contrast to ancient
Antibes, 7km north off the D103

lies one of France's newest towns,
Sophia-Antipolis. Though probably
not on most visitors' itineraries,
others would argue that this is the
Riviera of the future – a town of
high-tech industries which are
free to choose good international
communications and a superb
natural environment as the main
factors in their location. It has
attracted many of the leading
scientific and telecommunications
businesses, leading to inevitable
comparisons with California's
Santa Clara ('Silicon') Valley. More
than just a science park with
modern offices, the town has its
own banks and shops, sporting
facilities and even schools.

## ANTIBES, CAP D'

MAP REF: 113 F2

This is where the legend of the
summer Riviera was born, and
ever since F Scott Fitzgerald
recorded those early days in
*Tender Is the Night*, Cap d'Antibes
has attracted the most celebrated
and glamorous Riviera residents.
Inevitably their wish for
exclusivity has brought high walls
and private beaches, but there are
several places to visit, including
the Sanctuaire de la Garoupe, a

**Cap d'Antibes, where glamour and
wealth first became associated with
the Riviera**

**The Parc National du Mercantour nearly surrounds Auron**

chapel filled with sailors' ex-votos, and the Musée Naval et Napoléonien in the Batterie du Grillon, avenue J F Kennedy (despite Antibes' refusal to welcome Bonaparte after his escape from Elba to neighbouring Juan-les-Pins – see the Route Napoléon, page 64).

**For children** Four kilometres north of Antibes at La Brague (junction of the N7 and the D4 to Biot) is the greatest concentration of attractions for children on the Côte. It centres on Marineland, billed as the biggest in Europe, with an aquarium and daily performances by the inhabitants. Next door are Aquasplash water park, Butterfly Jungle, Antibes Land and La Petite Ferme Provençale, a re-created farm with animals and exhibits of local industries.

## AURON - ST ETIENNE-DE-TINEE

*MAP REF: 113 E3*

The oldest of the ski resorts in Alpes-Maritimes, Auron lies at 1,600m in the upper Tinée valley, almost encircled by the Parc National du Mercantour (see page 105). Though without its obvious winter attractions, Auron does host several sporting festivals in summer, and the Las Donnas *téléphérique* is open year-round, climbing to 2,474m and giving

panoramic views across the Tinée valley.

On the D39 to neighbouring St-Etienne-la-Tinée you can visit the chapels of St-Maur and St-Erige (which has the oldest fresco in the region), while St-Etienne itself has several other interesting chapels, including St-Sébastian with its remarkable 15th-century frescos and the 17th-century depiction of the Battle of Lépante in the Chapelle des Trinitaires. Walkers and hikers can find information on nearby walks from the Maison du Parc National in the Quartier de l'Ardon, St-Etienne.

St-Etienne has an important local sheep market, but you will need to be up early to catch the shepherds bringing in their flocks to be sold.
**Nearby** Forty two kilometres southeast, and 5km from the Italian border, Isola 2000 is the highest ski station of the Sud-Alpes, yet only an hour-and-a-half from Nice. A purpose-built village, it also promotes itself as a year-round resort, although it would perhaps make a better base for exploring the surrounding Parc du Mercantour than a destination in its own right, with the advantage that the hotels are cheaper off-season. The cable car here is also open throughout the year.

To reach the ski resort you must pass through the much older village of Isola at the confluence of the Rivers Guerche and Tinée near the Cascade de Louch, and roughly halfway between Auron and St-Sauveur-sur-Tinée, with its pretty

medieval church. Isola has a 12th-century steeple on the church of St-Pierre, and celebrates an annual Fêtes des Châtaignes (a festival of chestnuts).

## BAR-SUR-LOUP, LE

*MAP REF: 113 E2*

Apart from its superb natural setting in the Gorges du Loup, this small town's greatest attraction is man-made, and it is well worth exploring the maze of narrow streets to reach the 15th-century church of St-Jacques, from where there is a good view across the valley. Beyond its Gothic doorway lies an ornate altarpiece attributed to Louis Bréa (see La Brigue, page 91) and a curious 15th-century painting known as the *Danse Macabre*, which warns of divine judgement on sinners: dancers struck down by an archer (death) have their souls weighed in the balance of St Michael before being cast into Hell. The town is topped by the ruins of the castle of the counts of Grasse, the most famous of whom fought in the American War of Independence. Le Bar is also a good base for walkers, as several signposted circuits start from here.
**Nearby** Approaching Le Bar-sur-Loup from the north, the D6 follows the Gorges du Loup passing the Saut du Loup and the cascades, although the best views of the gorges can be had from the twisting D3 north of Gourdon, across the river.

## BEAULIEU-SUR-MER
### MAP REF: 113 F3

Once the smartest of the Riviera resorts, with an exceptionally mild climate, Beaulieu exudes old-fashioned charm, from its palm trees and casino to the stalwarts in four-star hotel elegance, the Métropole and La Réserve.

On the northern headland overlooking the Baie des Fourmis stands one of the Riviera's most fascinating museums, the Villa Kerylos, a remarkable reconstruction of a Greek villa built earlier this century by archaeologist Théodore Reinach. Once Reinach's home, it now houses a museum and foundation named for him, together with his collection of Greek vases, mosaics and statues (open every afternoon except Mondays and November; admission charge).

Serious swimmers can combine the benefits of seawater swimming in a heated pool with a visit to one of the traditional hotels of the Riviera at either La Réserve or the Métropole, whose pools are open to the public for a daily fee. If you prefer to get your exercise by walking, follow the Promenade Maurice-Rouvier south along the coast to St-Jean-Cap-Ferrat.

## BIOT
### MAP REF: 113 E2

Like Vallauris to the south, Biot (the 't' is pronounced) is a historic small town a few kilometres inland from the coast with a tradition of ceramic production which stretches back to Roman times. Since the arrival of Picasso, Vallauris has become better

**The harbour at Beaulieu-sur-Mer, a centre of wealth and of old-fashioned elegance**

known for its ceramics, but Biot has become synonymous with another great artist, Picasso's contemporary and fellow Cubist, Ferdinand Léger (1881–1955). A vast collection of Léger's work, donated largely by Nadia Léger, forms the basis of the Musée National Ferdinand Léger (one of the *département's* three national museums), housed in an appropriately imposing building southeast of the village. Beyond Léger's vivid mosaic set into the façade, the museum presents the perfect backdrop to his work, tracing its development from the impressionist influences to that of world war and the harsh depictions of man and industry in his later works, such as *Les Constructeurs.*

The village of Biot itself is charming: medieval gateways and sloping streets centre on the beautiful place des Arcades, best seen early in the morning or in the evening, as it is inevitably popular. If you happen to catch it open, the Musée d'Histoire Locale, next to the tourist office on place de la Chapelle, illustrates the history of the village through documents, costumes and possessions donated by local families.

One of the village's most ancient industries, ceramics, still flourishes here, with shops throughout the village and several workshops open to the public on the Route de la Mer, although glassware has taken over as the village's most famous product. One of the best places to watch glass-blowers at

work is *La Verrerie de Biot* on the Chemin des Combes. Other names to look for in the local galleries include Monod and Novaro.

## BREIL-SUR-ROYA
### MAP REF: 113 F3

Travellers with or without a car can reach the magnificent and remote Roya valley, and the tunnelling train trip from Nice is remarkable in its own right; however you get there, it is well worth the effort. Long-distance walkers can also follow the River Roya via the GR52A footpath from Sospel to Tende, the so-called Panoramique du Mercantour. Breil is a small town halfway between the high Alps and Ventimiglia, Italy, where the river joins the sea. It is literally 'on' the Roya, as it straddles the water (dammed at this point), and still looks to the river for its living and its leisure.

The old quarter is on the right bank, preserving its original medieval outline and many ancient façades. At its centre, the huge, imposing baroque church of Santa-Maria-in-Albis houses a variety of treasures, including an ornate early 16th-century altarpiece.

For a good insight into both the human and natural history of the region, visit the Ecomusée des Hautes Vallées de la Roya et de la Brévéra, one of the new breed of museums which can be found throughout France. *Ecomusées* aim to document the history and traditions of the people, their arts, crafts and means of production, as well as the local flora and fauna, in a lively and instructive way. This particular one can be found at the railway station (Gare SNCF), north of the town centre on the N204, where it presents exhibitions and videos in three disused railway carriages called the *muséotrain*. Olive trees have long been an important crop here, and several woodcarvers still practise their art in the old quarter of town.

Local produce is sold every Wednesday and Saturday morning on the place Biancheri, and there are regional fairs on the first Mondays in April and November. Every four years the inhabitants of Breil celebrate *A Stacada* (the next one is in 1994). This festival commemorates the famous revolt by local peasants against the understandably hated *droit de cuissage*, the local bailiff's feudal right to spend the wedding night with the bride of a serf. About a hundred locals dress in medieval costume to re-enact their victory, together with traditional dancing and an open-air public ball.
**Nearby** North of Breil, the N204 follows the Roya as it becomes increasingly narrow and, past the hamlet of La Giandola, enters the spectacular Gorges de Saorge, with great views of Saorge up ahead (see page 108).

**An old farmhouse in medieval La Brigue**

## BRIGUE, LA
### MAP REF: 113 F3

This charming village, set amid rolling pasture and beneath a ruined castle, lies a few kilometres east of the Roya valley, on its tributary, the Levense. Now with fewer than 700 inhabitants, the village has remarkable buildings as well as a superb view from the square west to Mont Bégo, the highest peak of the area, and overlooking the Vallée des Merveilles.

Medieval La Brigue was built of the local grey-green schist, including arcaded houses and the church of St-Martin. The church is remarkably ornate inside, with a fine restored organ, an early 16th-century work by the Italian Fuseri, and several works by the 15th-century primitive school. The Roya valley has some of the most important surviving examples of the so-called 'primitive' school of Nice painters led by Louis Bréa in the late 15th and early 16th centuries, famous for altar screens and frescos.

Perhaps the most renowned frescos of all are the vivid and macabre depictions painted by Canavesio and Baleison which cover the walls of the Chapelle de Notre-Dame-des-Fontaines, 4km east of the village. It is an essential side trip from La Brigue, across the magnificent Romanesque Pont du Coq, but check first at any hotel on the village to see if you will need a key. Notre-Dame-des-Fontaines is also famous locally as a centre of pilgrimage: there are processions held both on the saint's day and at Christmas Midnight Mass.

Away from the towns and villages, in the hillside pastures, look out for the *cazouns*, the shelters of the local shepherds, built of stone and camouflaged with grass.

## CAGNES-SUR-MER

### MAP REF: 113 E2

West of Nice and the industrial mouth of the Var, Cagnes-sur-Mer is a sprawling place with several distinct identities. The long resort strip of Cros-de-Cagnes runs on both sides of the N98, which continues past the region's main racetrack, the Hippodrôme de la Côte d'Azur. Here the winter season starts in December, but there are also evening meetings in July. The town itself, Cagnes-Ville, lies inland from the autoroute, forcing the River Cagnes to tunnel through its regimented path to the sea.

From the main square, the place Général de Gaulle, avenue Renoir leads east to the hills and the Domaine des Collettes, the home Auguste Renoir built in 1907. He spent his final years here, and despite his illness, it was a prolific period. The artist was inspired by the beautiful gardens, including a grove of ancient olive trees which his purchase of the estate saved from destruction. The 2.5 hectares are a haven of tranquillity, with some of Renoir's and Giono's sculptures as well as a rose garden and the little farm which was often the subject of his work. Inside, Renoir's *atelier* has been carefully re-created to be just as it was at the time when the artist worked there.

Furthest inland is by far the most attractive quarter: Haut-de-Cagnes, the original medieval village clustering around its château and restored to pristine, pedestrian-only perfection. Once home to a branch of the Grimaldi family, the handsome castle today houses a fascinating museum; exhibits range from local history through to modern masterpieces by artists who were inspired by the area. The Donation Suzy Solidor has 40 portraits of the singer by many of the same famous artists, and near by the *salle des fêtes* is decorated with a remarkable 17th-century *trompe l'oeil* – Carlone's *Fall of Phaeton*. And if you have seen the ancient olive trees at Les Collettes, you can also learn more about them here. From July to September the Château-Musée hosts its celebrated annual *Festival International de la Peinture*.

Outside, the place du Château is the scene of the daily Provençal market and a *brocante* market on Sundays. From the square, the Montée du Château leads to the chapel of Notre-Dame-de-Protection, with its 16th-century frescos and views to the sea.
**Nearby** Nine kilometres west across the dual carriageway D7, Villeneuve-Loubet is another ancient village with a medieval castle, although this one is not open to the public. Keen chefs and gourmands, however, will find ample compensation in a visit to the birthplace of Auguste Escoffier, now the Musée de l'Art Culinaire.

### THE ILES DE LERINS

A trip to either or both of the islands, accessible from Cannes, combines an interesting boat ride with a relaxing break from the resort: indeed, you may find that watching the town recede across the water is your ideal view of Cannes. Boats leave regularly from the Gare-Maritime next to the Palais des Festivals. Ste-Marguerite is best known for its Fort-Vauban, or royal fortress, a short walk to the left from the quay. Here the legendary Man in the Iron Mask was supposedly imprisoned; though most of the real prisoners held in these atmospheric stone cells were Huguenots. The fort also houses the Musée de la Mer, with well-presented archaeological exhibits. Fifteen minutes further from the mainland, St-Honorat is smaller and more peaceful, owned today by Cistercian monks, although the original abbey was founded by St-Honorat in the 4th century. You can visit the abandoned 11th-century fortified monastery on the headland between the abbey buildings.

**Haut-de-Cagnes, the restored old quarter of Cagnes-sur-Mer, huddling beneath its castle**

Le Suquet, the old quarter of
Cannes, rising above the beaches –
many of which are private (or
hotel) property

## CANNES

*MAP REF: 113 E2*

Cannes' history as a resort began
in 1834 when the English Lord
Brougham was forced to stay in
the small fishing village to the
west of cholera-stricken Nice. He
built a villa, Château Eléonore, and
returned every winter until his
death, while the port prospered as
one of the most fashionable on the
Riviera.

Today, Cannes is a resort with a
big reputation, but if film-star
spotting and designer-label
shopping aren't for you, there is
another side to this town which is
well worth exploring, too, though
you may want to avoid May, when
the International Film Festival
takes over.

The best way to get to know
Cannes is to stay overnight, and
then watch the town as it wakes
up. Orientation is straightforward:
to your left as you face the large
pink building which resembles a
multi-storey car park (the Palais
des Festivals; the car park is
underground) you can stroll along
the long sweeping seafront of La
Croisette with the early-morning
joggers; to your right, behind the
port, follow the rue Meynadier to
Les Halles and join locals and
yacht crews alike shopping for
fresh produce.

By mid-morning the beaches are
busy – and many are private.
Beneath the regimented rows of
palm trees, La Croisette itself is

neatly carved up between the
grand hotels whose roll-call
includes the Carlton, Majestic,
Martinez, Gray-Albion and the new
Noga-Hilton, though if you are as
happy to lie on the sand as on a
sun lounger, the corner of beach
in front of the Palais is public.
Serious shoppers in search of
portable famous names should
head to the streets between the
sea and the rue d'Antibes: the
Gray-Albion shopping mall offers
window shopping at a comfortable
temperature.

One of the best ways to escape
the midday sun is to explore
Cannes' oldest and most
picturesque quarter, the hill
known as Le Suquet, which rises
behind the western side of the
port. Le Suquet once gave an
important vantage point from
which to look out for Saracen
attack by sea, and fortifications
and a watch-tower were built by
the monks from the nearby Iles de
Lérins. Today Le Suquet still has
one of the best views around, and
the shady terrace below the tower
is a perfect place for a picnic. The
citadel itself houses a museum, the
Musée de la Castre, whose exhibits
range from local topography to
Asian and American arts. From the
watch-tower you can see southeast
to the two wooded Iles de Lérins,
the nearest and largest being Ste-
Marguerite and, behind, the
quieter St-Honorat.

**Nearby** Mougins, a perfect
Provençal village, with spectacular
views over Cannes only 7km away,
is unlikely to be a quiet,
unassuming place. Combine its
natural charms with some of the
region's top restaurants, such as

the nationally renowned Moulin
de Mougins, and you have one of
the most fashionable villages in
Provence. If you haven't come
here to eat, there is still plenty to
see, including an excellent Musée
de la Photographie in the old
Saracen gate ; the Musée d'Art et
d'Histoire on the place
Commandant-Lamy; and an art
exhibition space in the old village
*lavoir*, or washhouse. East of the
village via the D35 and D3, the
chapel of Notre-Dame-de-Vie
stands on a superb site (near
which Picasso chose to spend his
final years). A little further along
on the D3, the Musée de
l'Automobiliste has a huge, well-
presented collection of cars which
cover over a century of driving.

**Roman Polanski makes his mark:
one of the many stars' handprints
in the town that celebrates cinema**

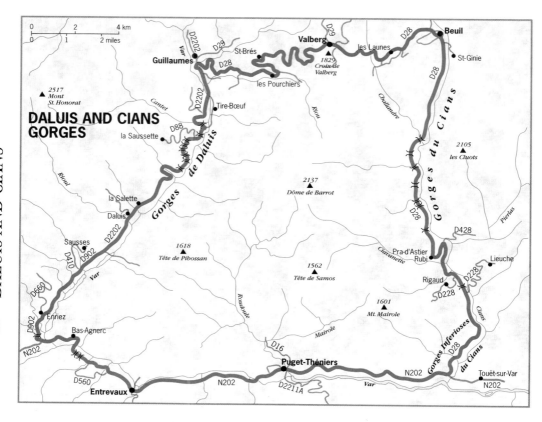

## DALUIS AND CIANS GORGES

(map labels, reading across)

0 2 4 km
0 1 2 miles

2517 ▲ Mont St. Honorat

D2202 • Guillaumes
Var
D29 • St-Brés
les Pourchiers
Valberg
1829 Croix de Valberg
D28
les Launes
D28 • Beuil
• St-Ginie

Cantel
D2202 • Tire-Bœuf
D88
la Saussette •
Riou
Chalandre
Gorges du Cians

2105 ▲ les Cluots

DALUIS AND CIANS GORGES

Gorges de Daluis
Rioul
la Salette •
Daluis •
D2202
2137 ▲ Dôme de Barrot
D28
Pierlas
D428

Saussses •
D410 D902
Var
1618 ▲ Tête de Pibossan
1562 ▲ Tête de Samos
Clavanette
Pra-d'Astier Rubi
Rigaud •
D228 • Lieuche
D228

D660
D902 • Enriez
Bas-Agnerc
N202
Roudoule
Mairole
1601 ▲ Mt. Mairole
Gorges Inférieures du Cians
Cians
D28
N202
Touët-sur-Var
N202

D560
• Entrevaux
N202
D2211A
D16
• Puget-Théniers
Var

---

## DALUIS AND CIANS

MAP REF: 113 E3

**The long and winding road: a pedestrian explores the route that follows every twist and turn of the spectacular Gorges du Cians**

## MOTOR TOUR

Though by no means as famous as the Grand Canyon du Verdon (see pages 64–5), the Daluis and Cians gorges are some of the most spectacular in Provence – and if you only make one trip into the heartland of the Alpes-Maritimes, there is no greater contrast to the resorts of the Riviera.

*The suggested starting point, Puget-Théniers, lies 54km northwest of Nice via the N202, and the tour itself is 83km (without any of the suggested detours).*
*NB In severe weather the road through the Gorges du Cians is closed. Check before starting out.*

### Puget-Théniers
This small and ancient town, which was once a Templar stronghold, stands at the confluence of the Rivers Var and Roudoule. The church dates from the 13th century, though it was remodelled some 400 years later. The sculpture in the elm-shaded square is by Aristide Maillol.
   Signs in the town direct you to the local Ecomusée de la Vallée de la Roudoule (follow the D16 to Puget-Rostang). Here a series of fascinating permanent and changing exhibits illuminate subjects such as local history, architecture, forestry, the fight against erosion and the remarkable

Louis Bréa altarpieces in nearby churches.

*Continue west on the N202 to Entrevaux, a remarkable town fortified by Vauban and lying just over the departmental boundary with Haute-Alpes-de-Provence.*

### Entrevaux
Like Puget-Théniers, Entrevaux (see page 67) lies on the Chemin de Fer de Provence, the narrow-gauge railway which runs between Nice and Digne-les-Bains. On weekends from May to October you can also ride the section from Puget-Théniers to Annot by a steam engine, known as the Train des Pignes.

*At the junction with the D902 to Guillaumes turn right. After 6km you recross into the Alpes-Maritimes, where the road becomes the D2202 and you enter the Gorges de Daluis proper.*

### Gorges de Daluis
Unlike most gorges, this one is not named for its river, which is the young Var. The village of Daluis lies off to the left of the road at an altitude of 700m, and is known locally for its Bressaou cheese, made from sheep's milk. Keen walkers can reach the Grotte du Chat via the path from the church. From Daluis the road becomes extremely twisty as it tunnels into

the dramatic red schist of the gorges, with plunging views over the Var and its cascades, cut into the green-stained rock.

*After 12km you reach Guillaumes.*

### Guillaumes
One of the main villages of the upper Var valley, Guillaumes is dominated by the ruins of the Château de la Reine Jeanne. In mid-August the villagers – who number just over 500 – celebrate the traditional annual feast by parading in the uniform of First Empire artillerymen. Visitors who enjoy something more exhilarating can try *saut en élastique* (bungee jumping) from the nearby pont de la Mariée. From Guillaumes you could continue further north on the D2202 to Entraunes, where the St-Sebastian Chapel has 16th-century frescos.

*Take the wooded D28 east and climb the 13km to Valberg.*

### Valberg
Standing at 1,669m above sea level, Valberg is the third most important ski resort in the Alpes-Maritimes.

Valberg lies on the GR52A long-distance footpath, and one-day guided hikes are organised by the Bureau des Guides et Accompagneurs. It could also be a base to explore the Parc National du Mercantour; behind the central plaza the Maison Valbergane has information on the park as well as being the local arts centre and cinema. Near by, the Chapelle Notre-Dame-des-Neiges has a surprisingly colourful interior; the saint's annual feast is celebrated every August. For the energetic, a climb to the peak of the Croix de Valberg, south of the village, will be rewarded by the best panorama of the surrounding mountains.

*Six kilometres east, turn right to enter the village of Beuil, another winter resort.*

### Beuil
At the centre of the village is an ornate 18th-century baroque church and a Chapel of the White Penitents, decorated with a *trompe l'oeil*. There is a children's festival in August.

*Continue south on the D28 to enter the Gorges du Cians.*

### Gorge du Cians
The dark red gorges are spectacular and a complete contrast to the Grand Canyon du Verdon (see pages 64–5), as here you are travelling at the bottom (rather than the top) of the precipice. There are several places where you can stop and admire the milky, dark pink waters of the Cians – most impressive at the Grande Clue and Petite Clue. These impossibly narrow clefts were once the only way to pass, but in the last couple of years they have both been by-passed by tunnels and the Clues can be explored on foot.

Sixteen kilometres from Beuil you can leave the valley to climb the tortuous roads to the tiny mountain villages of Lieuche and Rigaud. From here the red schist topped by green foliage changes dramatically to the grey-green limestone of the Gorges Inférieures.

*Rejoin the N202 8km east of Puget-Théniers. A short detour east leads past the tiny village of Touët-sur-Var, clinging to the side of the rocks.*

## EZE
### MAP REF: 113 F3
Just below the Moyenne Corniche, between Beaulieu and Monaco, the village of Eze clings to its rocky perch almost 500m above the sea below. Eze is Provence's most celebrated *village perché*, not as authentically medieval as it appears from a distance, but beautifully restored and with one of the most seductive viewpoints along the coast.

Whether you walk here or arrive by car, you will join hundreds of others in search of the picturesque, though everyone has to enter by the same 14th-century fortified gate.

If you can resist the galleries and boutiques *en route*, keep climbing until you reach the rue du Château and the Jardin Exotique. Only the ruins of the 14th-century castle remain now, atop gardens of cacti and succulents, and from here the panorama stretches from St-Tropez to Italy and, on a clear day, to Corsica. Below the château, on the place du Planet, the Chapel of the White Penitents is one of the few 14th-century buildings to survive intact. Inside are several crucifixes, including, on the altar, a smiling Christ from 13th-century Catalonia. The village's main church is more recent, rebuilt in the 18th century with a handsome façade and bell tower and rich baroque interior.

To reach the village on foot, take the train or drive along the Corniche Inférieur to the small resort of Eze-Bord-de-Mer. In summer there is a shuttle from here to the perched village, but a more energetic approach is via the Sentier Frederic-Nietzsche, a steep path signposted Le Village, which climbs through woodland to the place du Centenaire just outside the gate.

On the outskirts of the village the Parfumerie Fragonard has another factory (see Grasse, pages 96–7), a popular option for coach tours, where you can take a free guided visit which ends up, naturally enough, in the factory shop.

As well as the famous exotic garden, there is an exhibition of local flora and the forest at the Maison de la Nature in the Parc de la Grande-Corniche, open daily in season.

**Eze, a superb example of a Provençal perched village**

## GOLFE-JUAN
### MAP REF: 113 E2

If you plan to follow the Provençal section of the Route Napoléon – in the steps of the escaped Emperor on his march from Elba – then this sandy resort between Cannes and Juan-les-Pins will be your starting point. Napoleon landed in Golfe-Juan on 1 March 1815: on the quai du port an octagonal blue mosaic with the imperial eagle records the fact that *Ici debarqua Napoléon en 1815*. The eagle is the symbol that marks the route along its length – a reference to Bonaparte's reputed speech here about the eagle flying from steeple to steeple until it reaches Notre-Dame. The start of the route itself is marked by a plaque on the avenue de la Gare and, near by, a column which is topped by a bust of Napoleon.

If your intentions are strictly sedentary, Golfe-Juan still has much to recommend it, with a long, sandy beach, sea views framed by the Iles de Lérins to one side and the Cap d'Antibes to the other, and a new port complex with an occasional programme of live entertainment.

**Palm trees, white sands, deep blue sea... and sun-worshippers: Golfe-Juan, the starting point of the Provençal Route Napoléon**

## NAPOLEON'S ROUTE FROM GOLFE-JUAN

Bonaparte and his band of men tried first to win over Antibes. When they failed, they moved on to Cannes, where they camped near the Chapelle Notre-Dame de Bon Port – now replaced by Notre-Dame du Bon Voyage and with a marble relief on the north wall depicting that night of 1 March. From Cannes they marched via Mouans-Sartoux to Grasse, where they spent the second night on a plateau north of the town, now called the Plateau Napoléon. The next day, continuing northwest, they rested at St-Vallier-de-Thiey on the place de la Libération: the stone bench used by Bonaparte himself has been moved a few metres away, but its exact position in 1815 is marked by another column and bust. There are commemorative plaques of the troop's halts at Escragnolles and Séranon, where they spent the night, Napoleon himself staying at the Château de Broundet. On 3 March they made a stop at an *auberge* at Le Logis du Pin before arriving at Castellane (see page 64 for the Route Napoléon in the Alpes-de-Haute-Provence).

## GOURDON
### MAP REF: 113 E3

Perched high above the River Loup, 14km northeast of Grasse, the picture-perfect village of Gourdon has many undoubted natural assets, including a stunning view of the coast from its terrace. It calls itself the *nid d'aigles* (eagle's nest) a description that fits many of Provence's *villages perchés*. It has everything a tourist-seeking village should have – ancient church, inhabited feudal castle with museums open to the public, restaurants with views and the inevitable boutiques laden with the sights and smells of souvenir-Provence: lavender, olive wood, nougat, soaps and honey.

Although you can see the Mediterranean from the village, on a scorching summer day the splash of water on your skin can seem more impressive. Like many villages, Goudon has several fountains, but if you want to drink from one check first that it is *eau potable*, and not *non-potable*. Across from the château the fountain with the tall column is a popular place to cool off (but not to drink from). Look at the expressions on the faces of the four heads which spout the water into the pool.

Despite its peaceful air today, Gourdon was primarily a place of refuge and a stronghold of the Counts of Provence until the 13th century. The massive, squat castle which you can visit today was built in the 17th century and is still a private home. Inside are two museums: downstairs, the Museum of Medieval Art is the more interesting of the two, with a varied collection including paintings, furniture and some historic documents; upstairs is the Museum of Naïve Art. You must visit the downstairs section with a guide, but are free to explore the paintings at your own pace; afterwards you can wander among the immaculate hedges of Le Nôtre's garden and peer into the private part of the garden, complete with pool and tennis court.

## GRASSE
### MAP REF: 113 E2

The 'Balcony of the Côte', 'French Capital of Perfume', or, as it describes itself, 'Capital of Eastern Provence': despite a widespread reputation, at first sight Grasse is not a particularly attractive town, and it would be all too easy to leave knowing nothing more than the basics of perfume creation

distilled for you by one of the many perfumeries.

You will need to leave your car on one of the encircling boulevards to penetrate the steep streets and alleys at the heart of town. It is worth picking up a street plan from the tourist office on the place de la Foux (on the road to Nice), to find the daily market on the place aux Aires, the former cathedral of Notre-Dame-du-Puy with its paintings by Rubens and local artist Fragonard, and the Hôtel de Ville (formerly the Bishop's Palace) across the place du Petit-Puy. There's a good view of both the cathedral and the Pays Grassois from the small place du 24-Août next to the 13th-century clock tower.

Grasse has a cluster of good museums near the genteel place du Cours, the elegant face of the town which found popularity with the fashionable in the 18th and 19th centuries. That world is captured best in the Musée d'Art et d'Histoire de Provence in the 1771 Clapiers-Cabris mansion. Across the public gardens the Villa-Musée Fragonard commemorates the artist, not the perfume company. Jean-Honoré, the most famous painter in the family, spent very little time in Grasse and is one of three generations represented here. His father was a glove-maker, a profession linked inextricably with the rise of Grasse as a perfume

centre as well as tanning town after perfumed gloves became fashionable in the 16th century. If you want to know more about perfume you can choose between the International Perfumery Museum on the place du Cours and the free tours offered by the major companies, which inevitably end in the factory shop.

**Nearby** Six kilometres west of Grasse, Cabris is very pretty and very popular, a village dominated by its 17th-century church (with a polychrome wooden pulpit) ever since the 10th-century château was dismantled during the Revolution, though the ruins are still the place for views as far as the coast.

Like Grasse, the village of St-Vallier-de-Thiey lies on the Route Napoléon, but the natural landmarks around here go back to prehistory. There are several grottoes to explore, including the Grottes des Audides, the Grotte de Baume Obscure and the Grottes de St-Cézaire (remember to bring a sweater, as the temperatures underground will be chilly, however hot the sun is outside).

## JUAN-LES-PINS
### MAP REF: 113 E2

Although it has little history in the conventional – or pre-Riviera – sense, this fashionable resort across the Cap from Antibes has an interesting story as a *station de*

**Grasse is known as the French Capital of Perfume – but it has other attractions, too**

*mer*. It was born from nothing in the late 19th century, a plot of pine forest by the sea developed by a Cannes company, its name reputedly bestowed by one of Queen Victoria's sons. Juan-les-Pins did not really take off, however, until after World War I, when it was promoted as a summer as well as winter resort by railway tycoon Frank Jay Gould, and it acquired the glamorous and *risqué* image of its showbiz patrons.

The pines of its name are still evident and make a perfect backdrop to the annual International Jazz Festival, the town's most famous event, which takes over during the first fortnight of July. Throughout the rest of the summer (in winter it is much quieter), music continues to play an important role in the town's reputation as a late-night resort – the café orchestras play until the early hours, and shops stay open alongside clubs and the casino. If it seems that enjoyment is measured in decibels rather than in the quality of the beach, it is probably not the place for a holiday unless you plan to partake of the nightlife. The beach, however, is very attractive – a long, sheltered sweep of sand backed by the eponymous *pinède*.

## LEVENS

*MAP REF: 113 F3*

At the southern end of the Gorges de la Vésubie, Levens is an inviting small town with a medieval heritage – accessible from Nice, 22km to the south, and near to the dramatic scenery of the Vésubie and upper Var valleys. Climb to the very top of the town for the best views across the valley, or make the more challenging ascent of Mont Ferion via the Col du Dragon.

Visitors with an entomological bent can visit the Museum of Butterflies and Insects, with over 3,000 species. The Feast of Corpus Christi is celebrated with the 'procession of snails', when the streets are lit by tiny lamps made from snail shells.

**Nearby** The D19 north towards Lantosque follows the River Vésubie through its spectacular gorges, with a good viewpoint at the Bélvédere du Saut des Français. At St-Jean-la-Rivière, take the D32 for the long, looping climb to Utelle. This fortified medieval village has an interesting church and White Penitents' chapel, and lies a tortuous 6km from one of the most spectacularly sited sanctuaries in Provence – with views to go with it. Said to be the site of numerous miracles by the Virgin, La Madone d'Utelle has attracted the faithful and the curious since the 1st century: there are pilgrimages throughout the year, including Easter Monday, Ascension Day, Whit Monday, 15 August and 8 September.

## MENTON

*MAP REF: 113 F3*

Menton is best known for its lemons and for having one of the country's highest proportions of *retraités* ('retired' residents). If that doesn't sound like your ideal holiday destination, stop and think what those two facts might imply: year-round sunshine.

Menton certainly has the warmest winters on the Côte – the reason for its great popularity at the turn of the century with northern Europeans, many of whom came here for their health. Menton had only recently become part of France, bought along with nearby Roquebrune in 1860 from the ruling Grimaldis, after the so-called *villes libres* voted for freedom from Monaco. From the hilltop *vieille ville* above the curving Baie de Garavan, the town spread west along the Baie de Soleil with a series of grand hotels and, in the hills behind the town, some splendid villas and luxuriant gardens. The focus of town life shifted towards these broad new promenades and avenues with a casino – now the Palais de l'Europe, housing the tourist office and art exhibition centre (the newer casino is on the seafront) – and the long Jardins Biovès, which follow the course of the River

**Year-round sunshine ensures Menton's fame as a supplier of citrus fruits**

Careï. These gardens, lined with citrus trees and backed by the town's steeply rising mountainous windbreak, are the site of the famous annual Fête du Citron in February, when thousands of flowers, oranges and, of course, lemons are used to create gigantic models and tableaux.

If the now faded old hotels with their grand English names belie their former clientele, a more permanent reminder of those winter visitors can be seen in a visit to the Old Cemetery above the *vieille ville*, divided into separate sections for Menton's French, Russian, German and English residents who died here.

Menton is anything but dowdy today. It may not have the brashness or cachet of Cannes or Monaco, but it is certainly one of the most attractive of the Côte resorts, and the warm water off the sandy – and free – main beach can be an unbelievable luminous turquoise.

This area saw civilisation long before the 19th-century curists. A 30,000-year-old skull dubbed Grimaldi Man was found just across the border in Italy, and it now resides in the fascinating Musée Municipal de Préhistoire Régionale on the rue Loredan-Larchey. The star exhibit is also known here as Menton Man.

# TOWN WALK

A parking place can be hard to find in the compact centre of Menton, which is best explored on foot, though you may be lucky around the quai Bonaparte or the quai Napoléon III, which face the Baie de Garavan below the old quarter.

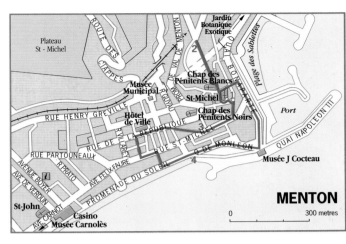

*Follow the quai Bonaparte towards the plage des Sablettes to the bottom of the flight of stone steps which climb up into the old quarter. After the first flight, cross the rue Longue, which was once the main street of the quarter, and continue to climb the double ramps to the parvis St-Michel.*

1 On two sides stand the elegant façades of St-Michel, with its ornate interior – particularly impressive when its pillars are draped with the traditional red hangings made of Genoese damask – and, opposite, the Chapel of the White Penitents. From these steps look back at the open side of the square, which on a sunny day is a stunning picture of azure water framed by terracotta walls and the black and white *parvis*.

Perhaps the best way to see the square is at night, during the internationally famous summer chamber music festival, when St-Michel becomes the backdrop and flickering torches line the stone staircase from the *quai* below. The square is blocked off to those without tickets, but if you cannot get them, join those who line the steps among the torches, where you can still hear the music.

*Take the small street on the north side of the square and continue to climb between and beneath the narrow, ancient houses to reach the rue du Vieux-Château and the Old Cemetery.*

2 Here Menton's once diverse population, who succumbed either to the charms of Menton or, often, to tuberculosis, rest separated by nationality, above another superb view of the old town and of the coast into Italy.

*Returning to the* parvis, *take the steep street between the two churches which leads down to the rue des Logettes and rue St-Michel, the heart of commercial Menton.*

3 This pedestrianised street bustles with life all day long, but there are several quiet corners, such as the place aux Herbes. Shortly after,

the street divides and the small place formed here is a popular spot for artists, musicians and mime artists in summer. Bearing right, away from the sea, will bring you to the rue de la République and the palm-shaded square by the Hôtel de Ville. On weekdays you can visit its remarkable Salle des Mariages, decorated by Jean Cocteau in 1957: if you have seen the St-Pierre chapel, which Cocteau painted in the same year at Villefranche, you will probably recognise his device of substituting a fish for the fisherman's eye.

*Head south from the square to rejoin the avenue Félix-Faure, the continuation of the rue St-Michel. To reach the casino and Jardins Biovès, turn right; turning left brings you back to St-Michel, where you can cut through any of the streets or squares off to the right to reach the large covered market and the Promenade du Soleil.*

4 At night, you will hear the clack of *pétanque* and the roars of some serious players along this stretch of the promenade. In the daytime, head toward the small bastion at the entrance to the harbour which houses more of Cocteau's works – and those of his contemporaries – in the Musée Jean Cocteau.

*From the Musée return to quai Bonaparte. Take the Promenade de la Mer to the northeast and stroll in the Garavan quarter, which still has many of its elegant villas and their gardens, including the Villa Isola Bella (short-term home to Katherine Mansfield) and Les Colombières, the former home of Ferdinand Bac.*

5 Below stretches the Jardin du Pian, a municipal park where outdoor concerts are performed

on summer evenings. Best of all for horticulturists is the Jardin Botanique Exotique on the avenue St-Jacques, in the grounds of Villa Val Rahmeh, which now houses a branch of the national Natural History Museum.

West of Menton along the avenue Carnot, the Musée Carnoles is the town's most elegant museum, filling the rooms of a palace which was once the summer home to the Monaco princes.

**A cupola on the Musée Jean Cocteau, which displays works by the artist and his contemporaries**

# •MONACO•

Immortalised in music hall song, Monte-Carlo's most notorious gambler was an English professional swindler, Charles Wells, who in 1887 'broke the bank' – or won the 100,000 francs with which the croupier had begun – 12 times in one day. At first Monte-Carlo society found Wells vulgar, but as news of his good luck spread he received invitations to the most exclusive parties, as well as hundreds of begging letters from those less lucky.

This tiny principality is famous for a variety of reasons: the lure of the casino, the roar of the world's most prestigious Formula One Grand Prix and the glamour of the ill-fated royal Grimaldis are well known. It is a truly theatrical place: row upon row of tower blocks crowd the hills around the central 'stage' of the harbour and lines of limousines still draw up before the casino every night. But even if you aren't participating in the action there is plenty to see and do without breaking the bank.

There are five distinct areas which centre on the deep, square harbour and central business district of La Condamine, which has an open-air public swimming pool on the sea-front. Arriving by sea you would see a rocky headland rising to the left – the old town of Monaco (map ref: 113 F3), or Monaco-Ville, where Prince Rainier III has his palace – and beyond that Fontvieille, a zone of newer development with marina, hotels and the huge stadium of AS Monaco football team. The slight headland to the right is Monte-Carlo, where the plushest hotels, historic casino and modern Palais des Congrès are at the centre of the flourishing business conference industry, and beyond that stretch the imported sands of the Larvotto beaches.

High in the hills behind Fontvieille, the Jardin Exotique is home to a remarkable collection of cacti and succulents of all shapes, shades and sizes. A global ticket is also good for admission to the Grottes de l'Observatoire, home of the prehistoric Monégasques, and to the Musée d'Anthropologique Préhistorique, where you can see their remains.

If picturesque Monaco-Ville is the historic seat of the Grimaldi authority, it is Monte-Carlo which really saved the principality. It is named for Charles III, the 19th-century Grimaldi prince who found himself ruling a greatly diminished land when Menton and Roquebrune declared themselves free towns and were sold to France in 1861. Without the income from Menton, Monaco faced bankruptcy, but within 10 years the money-spinning Casino and grand Hôtel de Paris were established under the *Société des Bains de Mer* and the new railway linked the fashionable resort with the rest of Europe.

Today, in place du Casino, the *Belle Epoque* still seems to be in full swing, although the best view of Charles Garnier's astonishing Casino and Opera is from the gardens on the seaward side. Below you are the angular lines of the Loews Monte-Carlo Hotel and the Convention Centre, whose roof features a giant multi-coloured mosaic by Victor Vasarély. Inside, the casino is just as spectacular: anyone over 21 with proof of age can visit the sumptuous gaming rooms, though you must pay to see beyond the American Room, where the ceilings get more extravagant and the stakes are higher.

Together with the refurbished Café de Paris and the grand Hôtel de Paris, this is Monte-Carlo's most splendid trio. Another of Charles Garnier's elegant buildings is Villa Sauber, on avenue Princesse Grace, now the National Museum of Dolls and Mechanical Toys. Today the principality has reclaimed more valuable land from the sea. Its self-promotion as an international conference centre has benefits for the visitor too, with a year-long calendar of festivals, sports championships and concerts.

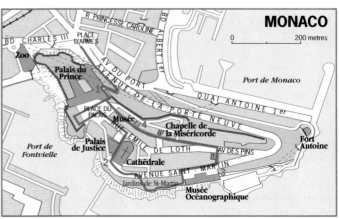

## TOWN WALK

The only way to explore the historic headland of Monaco-Ville is on foot. Here you will find most of the principality's museums, but if you plan to visit them all remember to budget for some steep entrance fees as well as the time taken.

*From the place d'Armes, the steep rampe Major climbs past spectacular views of La Condamine harbour and Monte-Carlo to the pretty place du Palais. If possible arrive in time to watch the daily ceremony of the changing of the guard at 11.55am.*

1 Dating in parts from the 13th to 16th centuries, the Prince's Palace is a creamy, mostly 19th-century confection, whose Louis XIV cannon and battlements are now purely decorative. From June to October you can take a guided visit of the sumptuous Grands Appartements beyond the 16th-century arcaded *cour d'honneur*. In another wing next door, the Museum of Napoleonic Souvenirs and Palace Archives has a vast collection of Bonaparte memorabilia.

*Take rue Emile-de-Loth. At the small square turn right, with the Palais de Justice on your right and the cathedral on your left.*

2 Dating from 1875, when it was built over an earlier church, the imposing cathedral of St-Nicolas is worth visiting for its exquisite 15th-century retable of St-Nicolas by Louis Bréa which stands to the left of the ambulatory, though most visitors come to see a 20th-century monument – the tomb of Princess Grace, which lies just beyond.

*Cross to the Jardins de St-Martin and follow the path on along the headland, rejoining the road at the Oceanographic Institute.*

3 With his new-found wealth earlier this century, Prince Albert I was able to finance his fascination with all things oceanographic and the institute which he founded now houses one of the most fascinating museums of the region. The prize of the museum is in the basement – the aquarium, with its extraordinary inhabitants!

*Opposite the museum an alleyway climbs to the place de la Visitation. Turn left, and take the*

*road to the right of the post office (rue Princesse Marie-de-Lorraine). Continue into rue Basse, passing the 17th-century Miséricord chapel.*

4 At 27 rue Basse the Historial des Princes de Monaco waxworks tells the story of the Grimaldis past and present.

## MOTOR TOUR

In the hills behind Monaco and Menton lie a series of perched villages which you can explore in a day.

*Leaving Monaco east via the Moyenne Corniche, start at Roquebrune.*

### Roquebrune
If you can, time your visit to coincide with one of Roquebrune's famous festivals, which have been celebrated since medieval times. Two re-enact the Passion on Good Friday, and again on 5 August in thanks for the village's deliverance from a 15th-century plague.

*A footpath and the D50 climb upwards to Gorbio. From the road down to Menton, turn left and head upwards again via the D22 to St-Agnès.*

### St-Agnès
There is also a footpath to this

very pretty, spectacularly situated village, which claims to be the highest on the Mediterranean coast.

*Continue on the scenic, but increasingly tortuous D22 west around Mont-Agel to a fascinating pair of villages.*

### Peille and Peillon
Dominated by its ruined fortress, Peille has a Musée du Terroir which commemorates the village's own distinctive dialect. It also has some interesting festivals: the *Fête du Blé et de la Lavande* (wheat and lavender) in early August, and the *Festin des Baguettes* on the first Sunday in September – celebrating not bread, but the olive branch which enabled a local shepherd to find the village spring and win the hand of his cousin (*baguette* literally means stick, hence the name of the loaf). If you are here in October, head on to the pretty village of Peillon and its beer festival (which you can also reach by train from Nice).

*To make this a circuit, return to Monaco via La Turbie, whose hilltop is crowned by the remaining pillars of Alpes-Maritimes' greatest Roman monument, the Trophée des Alpes. This 5th-century temple was built in order to commemorate the victory of Augustus over the rebellious tribes of the Alps.*

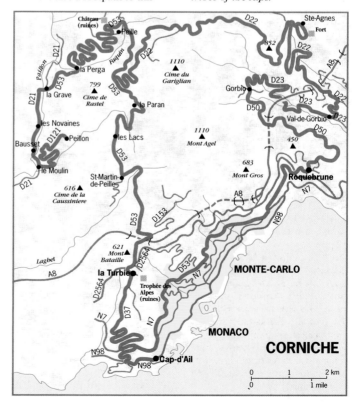

# • NICE •

France's fifth largest city can come as something of a surprise after its genteel neighbours. There is an enormous amount to see and do beyond the great sweep of the Baie des Anges, and it is worth taking time to orientate yourself to make the most of the markets, festivals and excellent museums which make this a colourful, year-round destination.

You can trace Nice's long history through the different areas of the city: excavations at Terra Amata in the hills to the west show that man was living here 400,000 years ago; across the harbour stands the rocky, now wooded hill known as the Château, topped first by the Greek acropolis and, much later, the château of the Dukes of Savoy. Roman settlement moved the city north to Cimiez, while medieval and Renaissance Nice (map ref: 113 F3) clustered around the base of the château hill between the sea and the River Paillon.

The triangular core of Vieux Nice, which you can explore on foot (see walk), still lies at the heart of the city, although the Paillon now runs its final course underground and it is a double sweep of boulevards with parks and fountains which separates the old quarter from the grid of 18th- and 19th-century streets. Nice's most famous landmark, the promenade des Anglais, was financed by the English residents to provide an easier access to the shore. The legacy of years as the western outpost of Savoy, facing French Antibes across the bay, has given Nice a distinct culture which you can hear and savour as well as see.

Nice today is a modern metropolis with its sights on the future. The traditional Carnival and Battle of Flowers in February may also be getting more commercialised, but there is plenty more to enjoy here. The new face of the city is most evident in the promenade des Arts – the broad curve of

parks, modern art museum, theatre and Acropolis – which sweeps up from the sea. Between the jets of the Espace Masséna and the established Jardin Albert-1er with its open-air theatre, the place Masséna is the city's main square – elegant, with dark pink stucco, despite the roaring traffic.

To the south the long strand of shingle and its broad promenade stretch on and on, the water dotted with swimmers and water skiers and the sky with the occasional paraglider, all under the impassive gaze of grand hotels and mansions.

North of place Masséna the pace is far from sedate: avenue Jean-Médecin leads past banks, department stores and the Nice-Etoile shopping centre, all jostling for position with street traders, fast-food restaurants and sleazy cinemas. Just beyond the SNCF station, where avenue Médecin becomes avenue Masséna, the tiny station of the Chemin de Fer de la Provence is the southern terminus of the narrow gauge railway which runs north to Digne.

A shopping trip to the hypermarkets to the east of the city can be combined with a visit to the Zygo-Parc, an amusement park with a variety of water rides on the Chemin de Crémat off the N202. The Muséoparc des Miniatures on boulevard Impératrice-Eugénie traces the history of the city from its beginnings at the *Terra Amata* through model buildings and wax tableaux (open daily, admission charge).

## MUSEUMS

Away from the beach, Nice's greatest attraction is its museums. Here is a selection; for a comprehensive list, ask at the tourist office at the airport, SNCF station or at 5 avenue Gustav-V. You should note that most of Nice's museums stay closed throughout November.

**Musée et Site Archéologiques**, avenue Monte-Croce, Cimiez (closed Sunday morning and Monday, admission charge); remains of the Roman arena and baths, together with a new museum, which brings *Cemenelum* to life through displays of discoveries at the site.

**Musée Matisse**, 164 avenue des Arènes-de-Cimiez (closed Sunday morning and Monday, admission charge); recently reopened after a major renovation, this is the artist's definitive collection. Matisse is buried in the cemetery of the nearby Monastère Notre-Dame.

**The Russian Orthodox Cathedral in Nice, built for its 19th-century colony of Russian aristocrats**

**Musée National Message Biblique Marc Chagall**, avenue du Docteur-Ménard (closed Tuesdays, admission charge); Chagall himself opened this specially commissioned building in 1972, which perfectly displays his series of 17 paintings richly illustrating the Old Testament, as well as sculpture, drawings and temporary exhibitions.

**Musée d'Art et d'Histoire**, Palais Masséna, 35 promenade des Anglais (closed Mondays, free admission); its exhibits range from magnificent First Empire furniture to the delicate watercolours of Niçois artist Emmanuel Costa.

**Musée Jules-Chéret**, 33 avenue des Beaumettes (closed Mondays, free admission); this is the city's Beaux Arts museum, with a range of works including Italian primitives, impressionists and local artists, all of which are housed in an extravagant mansion.

**Musée International d'Art Naïf Anatole Jakovsky**, avenue Val Marie (closed Tuesdays, free admission); another large villa, the Château Ste-Hélène, houses this extensive collection of works from the Art Naïf movement.

**Musée d'Art Moderne et d'Art Contemporain (MAMAC)**, Promenade des Arts (closed Tuesdays, free admission); part of the new concourse of culture, the structure is as intriguing as its exhibits.

**Terra Amata**, 25 boulevard Carnot (closed Mondays, free admission); this museum explores prehistoric Nice – an encampment of elephant hunters 400,000 years ago.

# TOWN WALK

The walk suggested here takes in most of the main monuments, but you could easily spend hours here exploring the maze of streets and alleys.

*Start in place Garibaldi.*

1 The statue of Giuseppe Garibaldi stands at the centre of this large, arcaded square with its merry-go-round: a native Niçois, Garibaldi was born in quai Lunel on the Port Lympia in 1807, when Nice was still under Italian rule. After becoming a member of Mazzini's Young Italy movement and leading a revolt in Piedmont in 1834 (which failed), Garibaldi made his name as a national hero during the 1848–9 Italian Revolution. His capture of Sicily and Naples helped bring about the unification of Italy in 1861.

*From the southwest corner of the square take rue Pairolière.*

2 The light open spaces of the 18th-century city give way to dark, narrow streets as you are drawn into the old town. Off to the left you can climb to the St-Martin-St-Augustin church, where Garibaldi was baptised and three centuries earlier Luther had celebrated mass. Busy rue Pairolière has a succession of small squares and fountains.

*Turn right into rue de la Loge, becoming rue St-Joseph, then climb the steps from rue Rossetti*

*to the Montée du Château.*

3 The chapel of St-Croix, on the corner, was that of the White Penitents. For those who cannot make the steep climb, there is a lift (*ascenseur*) on the south side of the château hill, near the Musée Naval. On foot you pass the large cemetery with its elaborate marble statues, next to a smaller Jewish cemetery, and at the top of the wooded paths there is a viewing platform and orientation table. Though the castle no longer stands, there are ruins and excavations to explore, including the city's 11th-century cathedral and remains of Roman and Greek Nice.

*Retrace your steps to the Montée du Château, then bear left via rue du Château and left again, to follow rue Jules Gilly to place Félix and the cours Saleya.*

4 St-Suaire is the chapel of the Red Penitents, but more imposing is the nearby Miséricord chapel of the Black Penitents – with a superb baroque façade and inside, if it is open, a 15th-century retable by Miralhet of the Nice School. The Musée de Malacologie has an aquarium and collection of shells from around the world, while art-lovers should make a short detour to see the Opera and the Galerie des Ponchettes on quai des Etats-Unis, which houses the Musée Dufy. As well as its daily fruit market, *brocante* on Monday mornings and flowers the rest of the week, the cours Saleya is a fashionable place for night-time dining.

*Take rue Gassin to the place du Palais.*

5 A fountain with unpredictable jets and sculptures from the nearby modern art museum set off the large elegant façade of the Palais de Justice and the Préfecture. More intimate is the small place Rossetti in front of Ste-Réparte cathedral, whose domed tower is clearly visible all over town.

*Take rue Rossetti to the junction with rue Droite and turn left, eventually rejoining rue Pairolière.*

6 At no 15 rue Droite, the Palais Lascaris is a rich museum behind an unassuming façade whose sumptuous apartments are filled with artworks contemporary with the 17th-century Genoese-style palace.

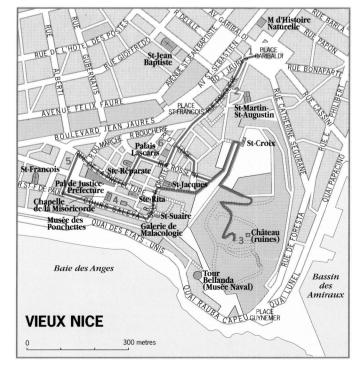

**VIEUX NICE**

0    300 metres

## ST-JEAN-CAP-FERRAT

*MAP REF: 113 F2*

Between Villefranche and
Beaulieu, some of the Côte's most
exclusive addresses sit on a
luxuriant peninsula tethered to the
mainland only by its long, slender
neck. Throughout its fashionable
history, Cap-Ferrat has been home
to kings, dukes and politicians, as
well as famous literary figures such
as Somerset Maugham, who lived
here in his villa La Mauresque for
nearly 40 years. Most of the villas
lie behind high clipped hedges,
and the peninsula would have
little of interest for the uninvited
visitor if it were not for one villa
where you are quite welcome to
roam the gardens and stare at the
Monets and the Renoirs. The
elegant, turn-of-the-century
italianate Villa Ile-de-France houses
the Musée Ephrussi de Rothschild.
The house and its rooms were
commissioned by Baroness
Ephrussi de Rothschild specifically
to display her vast collection of art
treasures. The villa's gardens are
laid out in English, Japanese,
Spanish, Florentine and, of course,
French style, complete with
statuary, fountains and a copy
of the Trianon's Temple of
Venus.

St-Jean itself is a small fishing
village-turned-resort, which is
surprisingly unexclusive. The
harbour faces east towards
Beaulieu and is dominated by its
large marina. If you want to swim,
the heated sea water pool at the
four-star Grand Hôtel du Cap is
open to non-residents for a daily
fee: cheaper for an hour or so is
the popular plage Paloma, east of
the port, on the Cap's own
peninsula of St-Hospice.

A well cared-for zoo and tropical

garden known particularly for its
chimpanzees and its butterfly
house stands just off the wide
bend where the boulevard
Général-de-Gaulle turns south.

## COUNTRY WALK

It is possible to follow a path right
around Cap-Ferrat, often between
private villas and the cliffs, but for
a shorter circuit with great views
back over the Beaulieu coast, St-
Hospice makes a good stroll.

*The footpath starts from plage
Paloma (take avenue Jean
Mermoz from St-Jean), leaving
the road which bears right to
follow the coastline.*

**A welcoming resort on an exclusive
peninsula, St-Jean-Cap-Ferrat has
been transformed from a fishing
village and now overlooks a
modern marina**

1 On the north-facing side of the
small peninsula you walk between
more concealed private villas and
superb, unhindered views of the
mainland, including, looking from
left to right, Beaulieu with its large
harbour, the hilltop village of Eze
and, beyond the small Cap d'Ail,
Monaco. The sweeping bay which
lies between you and Cap d'Ail is
called the Golfe de St-Hospice,
named for the saint who founded
an oratory on this then remote
spot.

*Walk round the Pointe de St-
Hospice and follow the south-
facing cliffs.*

2 The small white chapel which
stands here was built on the site
of the oratory and is now most
notable for its startling, enormous
metal sculpture of the *Virgin and
Child*. Also of interest here is
the small cemetery, where the
poignant neat lines of graves
are mostly of Belgian soldiers.
Outdoor concerts are given during
the summer months in front of the
chapel, which you can also reach
by road.

*The path continues south to the
Pointe du Colombier, where it
turns north, through a wooded
section following Les Fossettes
bay, until it rejoins avenue Jean-
Mermoz.*

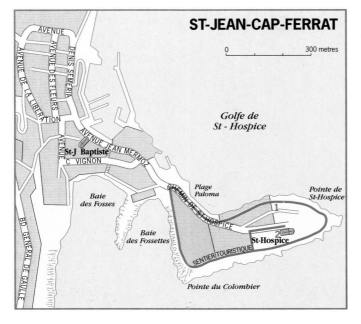

**ST-JEAN-CAP-FERRAT**

0 ——————— 300 metres

AVENUE
AVENUE DENIS SEMERIA
AVENUE DES FLEURS
AVENUE DE LA LIBERATION
AVENUE JEAN MERMOZ
St-J Baptiste
C VIGNON
BD GENERAL DE GAULLE

Golfe de
St - Hospice

Baie
des Fosses

Plage
Paloma

Pointe de
St-Hospice

CHEMIN DE ST-HOSPICE

Baie
des Fossettes

SENTIER TOURISTIQUE

St-Hospice

Pointe du Colombier

## ST-MARTIN-VESUBIE

*MAP REF: 113 F3*

In the corner of Alpes-Maritimes known as *La Suisse Niçoise*, mountain torrents cut through deep valleys, and the roads which follow them are steep and tortuous. The main village of the area, St-Martin-Vésubie, stands on the edge of the Parc National du Mercantour, where two of those mountain streams join to form the River Vésubie. It is an ideal base from which to explore higher into the mountains and the park. Serious walkers can consult the Mercantour Park office – on the main square across from the *mairie* – or the Bureau des Guides for trail suggestions, while the less adventurous can unwind amid spectacular scenery and explore the ancient village itself.

The original main street, rue Dr-Cagnoli, is narrow, steep and cobbled, and the water conduit running down the middle may catch out the unwary. From the main square, place Félix-Faure, it runs down past a chapel of the White Penitents, the Guides' office and some ancient and imposing houses, towards the church of St-Martin and views over the rushing stream of Madone de Fenestre. Inside the church you can see part of a Louis Bréa altarpiece and, from October to June, the richly decorated medieval wooden statue of Notre-Dame de Fenestre. During the summer, the statue resides in the chapel of Madone de Fenestre, 21km upstream: the procession there and back and the monthly summer pilgrimages are the main reasons to make the long and

**St-Paul-de-Vence, a 16th-century hilltop village**

steep trip. Experienced walkers could follow the GR52 (long-distance footpath) west from here to the lake, beautiful cascade and small village of Le Boréon – but even by car, the 8km from St-Martin can be testing enough. Hikes ranging in length and difficulty leave from here towards Mont Mercantour and its lake, and several peaks across the Italian border at over 3,000m.

### THE MERCANTOUR NATIONAL PARK

St-Martin is one of many bases from which you can explore the Mercantour National Park, and, at its centre, the famous Vallée des Merveilles: over 40,000 carvings, dating from 1800BC, of weapons, figures and geometric patterns etched into the rock in the Fontanalbe and l'Arpette valleys at the foot of remote Mont Bégo. Once you reach the valley, visitor access to this classified historic monument is limited, and without a park guide the engravings can be hard to find. Summer walking tours are offered by the *Bureau des Guides et Accompagnateurs* in Tende. The park is home to a variety of wildlife, including the chamois, mouflon and marmot, birds of prey, including several nesting pairs of golden eagles, and alpine plants.

### ST-PAUL-DE-VENCE

*MAP REF: 113 E2*

A complete ring of 16th-century ramparts keeps this medieval and Renaissance village safe from the

modern villas which dot the green slopes below. Though not the highest, St-Paul-de-Vence is certainly the epitome of Provence's hilltop villages. Thirty or 40 years ago, the undeniable beauty of the narrow streets and the extraordinary local light attracted many then unknown artists, who lodged, for the payment of a canvas, at the local inn, La Colombe d'Or, leaving the present owners with an almost priceless collection. Lunch among the likes of Mirò, Léger and Utrillo here, however, is but an appetiser for the world-famous collection on the hill of la Gardette outside the village. The Fondation Maeght is one of the most important, and enjoyable, collections of modern art in the world and should certainly figure in any art-lover's itinerary of this part of Provence.

Beyond the north gate and the tourist office the main street, rue Grande, leads past boutiques, art galleries, restaurants and yet more art galleries to the south gate at the far end. Back at the centre it is a short climb from the elegant urn fountain to the small place de la Castre, where the church presents a solid, plain exterior in contrast to the rich decoration within.

Across the square, the former 12th-century keep now houses the town hall and a small museum of local history whose tableaux of wax figures depict important episodes in St-Paul's early history. One of those figures, François I, was responsible for the building of the ramparts to protect what was then the French border from neighbouring Savoy. You can still walk around them and explore those back-streets of the village, where the houses have yet to become boutiques.

ST-PAUL-DE-VENCE

105

# ·WINTER SPORTS·

Originally known as a place to go to escape the British winter, Provence has in more recent times become popular as a summer destination. So popular, in fact, that in July and August the Riviera is uncomfortably crammed with sun seekers. But now, more and more people are realising the potential of a winter break in the South of France linked to some activity, particularly snow sports. And the opportunity to ski on the slopes of the high-altitude Hautes-Alpes, in the wild valleys of the Alpes-de-Haute-Provence or on the sunlit Alpes-Maritimes, has proved irresistible to many.

Skiers gather at the British-built
Isola 2000 resort

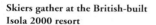

## SKIING FOR ALL THE FAMILY

French ski resorts are becoming more and more popular, for two very good reasons. First, most of them have been built with the needs of the skier in mind – you can literally ski down to your own front door and be sure that there are adequate facilities for drying clothes or storing your skis without cluttering up your room. And most places offer a choice of hotels or other accommodation equipped to a very high standard, with washing machines, dish-washers and television. These are particularly popular with families, for there is always somewhere on the spot where you can buy ready-cooked meals and a good supermarket to keep costs down. Restaurants offer a full range of food and prices, from crêperies and snack bars to highly rated gourmet establishments. All kinds of activities are available by day, from skating to snow walking and hiking, and the night life is lively too. Children are always well catered for, with their own club and crèche, and other events arranged specially for them.

The second advantage of French ski resorts is that they are lavishly equipped. You can be sure there will be the newest and most efficient machinery for getting you up to the higher slopes quickly and effortlessly and for keeping pistes in perfect condition. If snow is a bit thin on the ground, more can be created with the help of snow guns.

## SUN AND SNOW

Of all the ski resorts in France, the Alpes-Maritimes offer the best mix of sun and snow. Indeed, if you choose somewhere near the Mediterranean coast, you can literally be sunning yourself in the morning and skiing in the

afternoon. The best-known place that comes under this category is the British-built resort of Isola 2000, so called because of its altitude of 2,000m. Just 94km from Nice, and ultra-modern in its construction, it offers a wide range of accommodation, with 44 pistes for skiers to choose from and 23 ski lifts. Isola has three main skiing areas – the Domaine du Pélévos, the Domaine du St-Sauveur and the Domaine du Levant – offering between them every conceivable grade of skiing from total beginner up to the highest Olympic standard.

For more sunshine with your skiing, Auron is another burgeoning resort, 90km from Nice. At an altitude of 1,600 to 2,450m, it has 10 hotels to choose from with a further five at St-Etienne-de-Tinée. Auron offers a choice of five main ski areas, and après-ski includes films, ice skating and the usually boisterous French night life. Also not far away – and a particularly good place for beginners – is Valberg, 85km from the coast. More resorts in the Alpes-Maritimes – Super-Dévoluy, for instance – offer the same cocktail of sun and snow. Super-Dévoluy has over a hundred kilometres of pistes, plus another 44km for cross-country skiing. If you want to tune in to the atmosphere of typical old Provence, then stay at the village of St-Etienne-en-Dévoluy near by.

Further north is Barcelonette, Provence's most northerly town. It makes an intriguing centre for skiing in the Alpes-de-Haute-Provence, an area less crowded than the better-known south. Le Sauze and Super-Sauze are two resorts worth trying. In the same vicinity is La Foux d'Allos, an up-and-coming place set at 1,800 to 2,600m. It has 160km of piste to ski on and is less crowded than the better-known resorts. Although relatively new, La Foux d'Allos is built in traditional style. There's a children's club, a ski school and plenty of night life available – and it gets about 300 days of sun every year.

Another lesser-known place worth going to is Chabanon, near Seyne-les-Alpes, north of Digne. This small family resort is set in 1,000 hectares of forest with powder snow, usually from December to May. Further west in the Vaucluse, there is skiing on Mont Ventoux; you can choose between the traditional downhill on its slopes or cross-country. It is based on Mont Serein, Ventoux's second highest peak at an altitude of 1,445m.

## COASTAL RESORTS

If you prefer sand to snow – although some coastal resorts virtually close down out of season – places like Nice, Cannes and Menton are all seeing a big revival in winter tourism and have programmes very much on a year-round basis. Midwinter offerings include opera music, casinos and restaurants.

If you have a car (and winter fly-drive packages are worth investigating), out-of-season is a good time to do some sightseeing, when fewer fellow tourists are about. There are the hill villages of Roussillon, Bonnieux and Gordes in the Lubéron, and Vence and La Turbie on the Riviera to choose from. You can also visit museums and art galleries like the Fondation Maeght at St-Paul-de-Vence on the Côte d'Azur when they are less crowded, and explore cities like Avignon and Marseille. There's always something going on: the Foire des Santons at the end of December in Marseille, the Monte-Carlo Rally at Cannes in January, the pre-Lenten carnival at Nice.

## RAMBLING AND WALKING

Another winter activity that's becoming more and more popular is *randonnée*, or rambling. No one wants to toil over hilly terrain in soaring summer temperatures, but out of season it can be an exhilarating experience. You can buy IGN *Topo* guides in French, which trace the footpaths over the countryside, while the paths themselves are marked by two types of distinctive signposts: red and white for long-distance walks, yellow for shorter ones. The best areas to explore are in the Vaucluse – the Colorado, for instance, a range of ochre cliffs that are less well-known than those at Roussillon. The lower slopes of Mont Ventoux and the Dentelles de Montmirail all have well-marked footpaths. For keen riders, the place to go is the Camargue, where horse rental is easy and there are many interesting tours and horse-treks on offer.

Climbing, too, is done out of season. One of the most fascinating places to visit is Buoux, near Apt in the Lubéron, where climbers from all over the world – particularly Japan – take on the almost sheer rockface of a range of cliffs overlooking a deep valley.

Mountain biking is another sport that is becoming increasingly popular, and bikes can be rented in all major towns. There's no excuse for boredom in this corner of France, whatever the season.

The Trophée des Alpes, La Turbie

## SAORGE

*MAP REF: 113 F3*

On the approach from the south, Saorge's dramatic setting seems unreachable, but for those who enjoy a challenge it is certainly worth exploring. The easiest approach is to continue north on the N204 and turn off at Fontan, a village which similarly features the distinctive red and purple stone roofs of the area. Steep, twisting streets and alleys lead to a trio of ecclesiastic buildings: the church of St-Sauveur with one of the valley's best organs (see Breil-sur-Roya, pages 90–1), a 17th-century Franciscan convent with rich frescos and views over the village, and, via a path from the village, the Romanesque church of Madone del Poggio.

## SOSPEL

*MAP REF: 113 F3*

The D2204 from Nice and the D2566 from Menton head north into the mountains to meet in the Bévéra valley at the small market town of Sospel. If you are travelling south, however, from the dramatic and remote Gorges du Piaon or from the Vallée de Roya, this village with some 2,500 residents can seem quite a metropolis. It is worth the trip, in either direction, as it is an ideal base for exploring the area, particularly for walkers, and while it has none of the pretensions of prettier villages further south, Sospel has one of the most handsome small squares in the Alpes-Maritimes.

The most immediate point of interest is the tollgate, a reminder of its past importance, in the middle of the 11th-century bridge over the Bévéra, the Pont-Vieux, straddling what was then the only route between Nice and Piedmont. Cross to the left bank to see the fountain on the place St-Nicholas, and then recross via the Pont de la Libération for a view of the tollhouse and the rock-strewn waters of the lazy Bévéra. From the small square facing you, the rue St-Michel leads to the town's main showpiece, the place St-Michel, and its perfect ochre and apricot baroque ensemble.

The two small chapels to the left of the former cathedral of St-Michel are those of the Red and Grey Penitents, and opposite stands the beautiful façade of the town's finest house, the Palais Ricci. The bell tower of St-Michel is 11th-century. But it is inside that the church is really remarkable: a vast space which is totally unexpected from the dimensions of the façade.

As well as its size, the church has many treasures to explore, including an ornate baptismal font, a 17th-century Notre-Dame-de-Bon-Voyage and a superb Bréa altarpiece depicting the Blessed Virgin.

**Nearby** North of Sospel, the Piaon Gorges make for dramatic driving, with breathtaking scenery and a tiny chapel with one of the most superb settings in Provence. Notre-Dame-de-la-Menour, a pretty Renaissance building, can be seen from a distance, looking out over the great chasm of the gorge from its rocky perch. It can be reached via a sweeping flight of steps.

## COUNTRY WALK

This easy circular walk of 4km to an underground fortress of the Maginot Line will take about an hour and a half. Approaching by car, the fort lies off the D2204 south of the town.

*Start from the place de la Cabraia in Sospel.*

The name 'Cabraia' comes from the word for 'nanny goat'. Take a look at the fountain here and you will see that it has two levels: the lower one was used by the townsfolk's goats before being taken up to communal pasture every morning by the town goatherd.

*Take the rue Comiti and rue Auda around behind the cathedral, bearing sharply right before meeting the D2204 from Nice. Turn left and cross the railway line, following the west wall of the cemetery, then cross the road and take the path (with red and white markings) off to the right.*

After a looping climb of about 15 minutes (barely visible at the beginning), the path arrives at a small plateau with olive trees known locally as La Coletta. Here the path widens and joins a tarmac road to the Ranch de Jonathan. A couple of detours for longer, steeper walks are possible near here: the first, a climb to the Col de St-Jean (7.5km), leaves from the road to the right. The second and arrowed path to the 847m peak of Mont Barbonnet and its fort, is signed about 450m off the path to Fort St-Roch, which continues to the left here. Fort Suchet on Mont Barbonnet also has a museum.

*Thirty-five metres after the Mont Barbonnet path, turn left to follow the yellow arrow which soon rejoins the Circuit des Tourelles and drops down to the platform at the entrance to Fort St-Roch.*

The secrets of Fort St-Roch lie deep underground. It was built in 1932 to withstand the Italian advance, with 1km of galleries, a periscope, an electricity generator and kitchens to serve 230 soldiers. Now, as a museum, it is an evocative memorial to the horrendous battles which took place around Sospel when the now tranquil southwest Alps were ravaged by both Italian and German troops.

*The path from the fort continues to descend, joining the tarmac path, until you reach the cemetery on your right. Recross the railway line and return towards the rue Audra, but turn right on the rue de l'Abbaye, beneath the castle ruins. Either take the stepped alley down into the place St-Michel, or continue past the ivy-covered tower to the communal wash house, or lavoir.*

## TENDE

MAP REF: 113 F3

Like Saorge, Tende did not officially become part of France until 1947, and it too has long played a strategic role guarding the Roya Valley and the Nice-Piedmont mountain route. The jumble of horizontal layers of houses and occasional vertical bell towers hugs the valley side, topped by more layers of terraced tombs in the town cemetery – an ever-present reminder of mortality.

## ARCHITECTURE OF THE ROYA VALLEY

As well as having two of the best organs of the Roya Valley in the Collégiate Church and Chapel of the Black Penitents, Tende shares the distinctive architecture of the *pays*. This includes *trompe-l'oeil* painted façades which can be seen on the presbytery in Tende, the church in St-Dalmas and many other buildings, as well as the colourful roofs of the region. While towns nearer the coast have tiles, those higher up tend to have sturdier stone slabs *(lauzes)* which vary in colour depending on the local rock, from purples and reds in Saorge to greens at Tende. The ochre colour of many buildings is due to the plastering, another form of added protection against the harsher elements in the mountains.

**Colourful houses perched high up in the village of Saorge**

## VALLAURIS

MAP REF: 113 E2

The local reverence for Picasso is taken to extremes in Vallauris. His interest in clay and the work of the Madoura studio has left a legacy here which includes the bronze statue of *L'Homme au Mouton* in the market place, and a great collection of the artist's work in the Musée Nationale de Picasso and Musée de la Céramique et d'Art Moderne, not to mention a now flourishing ceramic industry.

The municipal museum is excellent, housed in the handsome Renaissance castle on the place de la Libération, with a broad collection of ceramics and the remarkable works of Alberto Magnelli as well as pieces by

**A bridge from the past: Sospel's 11th-century Pont-Vieux, spanning the Bévéra**

Picasso. Across the courtyard, Picasso painted his mural *La Guerre et la Paix* in the small vaulted 12th-century chapel. It has long been deconsecrated, but there is still something slightly unsettling about the large portrait of Picasso hanging where the altar once was.

The main street which climbs up to the place de la Libération is lined with galleries and ceramic shops. Market-hunters will find traditional Provençal stalls in the morning on place Paul-Isnard, across from the museums, and an indoor *brocante* and flea market just off the place de la Libération (closed on Sundays).

## VENCE

*MAP REF: 113 E3*

Like many towns in Provence, Vence can trace its history back beyond the Romans, and its fascinating medieval quarter, the Cité Historique, is well-preserved within an encircling ring of houses pierced by gateways. There are still traces of Roman Vence to be found throughout the town, including a pair of columns presented by the Republic of Marseille (as it then was) early in the 3rd century.

Just before you enter the gateway, the place du Frêne is distinguishable by its ancient ash tree *(frêne)* standing before the 16th-century château of the Villeneuve family, now home to the Fondation Emile Hugues and the Musée Carzou, with a wide collection of works by this contemporary artist. Inside the Cité, the elegant urn-shaped Fontaine de Peyra is one of Vence's most photographed corners. The present fountain dates from the 19th century. The rue du Marché leads to the central square, the place Clemenceau, which has seen many changes: the cathedral with its jumble of ages and styles stands on the site of the Roman temple, and the pretty, slightly incongruous Hôtel de Ville was built earlier this century over the old Bishop's Palace.

Upstairs in the cathedral, and certainly worth investigating if it is open, the organ loft and choir stalls are richly carved; downstairs, look for the mosaic by Marc Chagall. From the east door you can step into the other sizeable square of the old quarter, the place Godeau, named for another of Vence's famous bishops. The streets of St-Lambert and St-Véran each lead from the square to gateways in the Cité walls: take St-Lambert to see the more interesting 13th-century Porte Signadour, and also the place Surian, where you can go shopping along with the locals at the daily market.

There is plenty to explore outside the Cité too. The most visited monument in Vence is the small Chapelle du Rosaire north of the town centre on the St-Jeannet road (D2210). Also known as the Chapelle Matisse, it is named for the artist who in the late 1940s combined white tiles, bold, black lines and bright blue, yellow and green stained glass to create a stunningly simple interior. At 3 Descente des Moulins the Centre Culturel Henri Matisse is a converted olive oil mill with changing exhibitions of sculpture, paintings and photography. Slightly further from town, the poetic-sounding Château-Notre-Dame-des-Fleurs, just off the road to Grasse, is a good introduction to the sights and sounds of the perfume industry ahead. Originally a Benedictine abbey and later the residence of the Bishops of Vence, today it houses the Musée du Parfum et du Liqueur.

**Nearby** The *pays Vençois* includes some of the highest peaks in the region, including the Montagne de Cheiron at 1,777m and the Audibergue ridge which reaches 1,642m. Less strenuous excursions by foot or by car will be rewarded with superb views towards the Cité Historique and across to the sea (footpaths are well signposted). For the best views, take the D2 to the Col de Vence, passing the ruined Templar castle *en route*. The local rocky outcrops, known as *baous*, are well worth exploring: turn off the D2 on to the Chemin du Riou to reach the Grotte du Riou – the spring supplying Vence's water – and a footpath to the Baou des Noirs.

## VILLEFRANCHE-SUR-MER

*MAP REF: 113 F2*

Despite its prime Côte location, this small resort, for which the *rade* (harbour) is named, has retained the atmosphere of a historic, if exclusive, fishing village, and behind the harbourfront of pink and ochre façades, a maze of narrow streets, squares and stepped alleys can only be explored on foot. Between the port and the pleasure harbour to the west rise the solid walls of the 16th-century Citadelle St-Elme, which now shelters an open-air theatre, the Hôtel de Ville and several art collections. These include the Volti Foundation (copper, bronze, terracotta and stone sculpture), the Goetz-Boumeester Museum of paintings, the Roux Museum of historic ceramic figurines, and changing exhibitions in the St-Elme Chapel, as well as a small but fascinating museum of underwater archaeology.

Between the steep walls of the citadel and the ocean, a path leads around the quayside and the small St-Pierre Chapel, decorated by Jean Cocteau in 1957 in dedication to local fishermen and their patron saint.

**Pottery on display in a Vence shop**

## Map symbols

|  |  |
|---|---|
| A4 | Motorway - dual carriageway |
| A7 | Motorway - single carriageway |
| A1 | Toll motorway - dual carriageway |
| A6 | Toll motorway - single carriageway |
| | Motorway junction |
| | Motorway junction restricted access |
| | Motorway service area |
| | Motorway under construction |
| | Primary route |
| | Main road |
| | Secondary road |
| | Other road |
| D600 E57 N59 | Road numbers |
| | Dual carriageway or four lanes |
| | Road in poor condition |
| | Under construction |
| TOLL / Toll | Toll road |

|  |  |
|---|---|
| | Scenic route |
| )=========( | Road tunnel |
| 68 | Distances (km) |
| 10·6 / 970 | Mountain pass (height in metres) with closure period |
| | Gradient 14% and over. Arrow points uphill |
| | Gradient 6% - 13% |
| | Frontier crossing with restricted opening hours |
| ---V--- | Vehicle ferry |
| | Airport |
| | International boundary |
| | Viewpoint |
| | Motor racing circuit |
| 2973 DIAVOLEZZA | Mountain / spot height in metres |
| | Urban area |
| | River, lake and canal |
| ■ Jockfall | Place of interest |
| | Mountain railway |
| | Car transporter (rail) |

# PRACTICAL GUIDE

Artists great and small are still drawn to Provence

## Conversion Table

| From | To | Multiply By |
| --- | --- | --- |
| Inches | Centimetres | 2.54 |
| Centimetres | Inches | 0.3937 |
| Feet | Metres | 0.3048 |
| Metres | Feet | 3.2810 |
| Yards | Metres | 0.9144 |
| Metres | Yards | 1.0940 |
| Miles | Kilometres | 1.6090 |
| Kilometres | Miles | 0.6214 |
| Acres | Hectares | 0.4047 |
| Hectares | Acres | 2.4710 |
| Gallons | Litres | 4.5460 |
| Litres | Gallons | 0.2200 |
| Ounces | Grams | 28.35 |
| Grams | Ounces | 0.0353 |
| Pounds | Grams | 453.6 |
| Grams | Pounds | 0.0022 |
| Pounds | Kilograms | 0.4536 |
| Kilograms | Pounds | 2.205 |
| Tons | Tonnes | 1.0160 |
| Tonnes | Tons | 0.9842 |

## Arriving

**Entry formalities**
You only need a passport to enter France if you are a citizen of an EC country, the Council of Europe (except Turkey), the US, Canada, Japan, Australia and New Zealand; citizens of other countries need a visa as well, but check before your visit with the French Consulate to see whether the situation has changed.

**By air**
International flights arrive at both Marseille and Nice-Côte d'Azur airports. Scheduled services between Britain and Nice are operated by British Airways, Canada, Air UK, British Midland and Air France. Unless you are renting a car at the airport, take the bus into Nice-Ville for the SNCF station, or express buses direct to other coastal destinations.

**By rail**
Train travellers using InterRail passes – now available to travellers of any age – can arrive in Provence in style on the *Train à Grand Vitesse*, or TGV. Paris to Nice takes 7 hours, and in summer there are three trains daily. If you prefer to take your own car but want to avoid the long drive south, SNCF motorail services operate from Calais to Nice, with additional summer services to Provence from Boulogne and Dieppe.

**By road**
The *Autoroute du Soleil* is notorious in summer for accidents, but the A6 from Paris, becoming the A7 south of Lyon, is undoubtedly the fastest route to Provence, with the A8 heading east to the Côte d'Azur just north of Marseille. To avoid some of the traffic (especially the last weekends of July and August and around the feast of the Assumption on 15 August) as well as the tolls, the N7 is a good alternative; it reaches Lyon via Moulins, then criss-crosses the A7 and the Rhône south to Aix, where it follows the A8 to the Italian border.

## Camping

There are many camping sites throughout Provence, graded from one to four stars according to the facilities on offer. The best have a restaurant, shops and swimming pool on site. Other options include *campings à la ferme* and *aires naturelles de camping*, usually small, simple sites with few facilities. You can obtain lists from branches of the French Government Tourist Office or local tourist offices.

## Crime

A stolen wallet or purse can ruin a holiday and if you are a victim of crime the chances are it is because you are a tourist. Avoid being conspicuous, particularly in the larger cities on the coast. Use a moneybelt or keep your bag strapped across your body, and don't leave valuables on show in your car – foreign licence plates are particularly attractive to potential thieves. Above all, don't take something that you couldn't bear to lose. Report any theft to the local *gendarmerie* immediately and get a signed note for your insurance claim.

## Disabled Travellers

Independent travellers should contact their nearest French Government Tourist Office for advice and also consult guides such as the *AA Guide for the Disabled Traveller*. Wheelchair-bound visitors will need help to negotiate the steep, cobbled streets of many Provençal towns. Hotels can also present a problem, as they are often in old buildings with steep steps and narrow doorways. Hotels (and campsites) suitable for disabled visitors are indicated in tourist office lists.

## Driving

Apart from driving on the right, the main rule to remember is *priorité à droite* (priority to the right), though this is usually overruled on main roads with *passage protégé* (except in built-up areas) and on roundabouts (*rotaries*), where a sign indicates that *vous n'avez pas la priorité* (ie you must give way to traffic which is already on the roundabout).

Speed limits, reduced in wet conditions, are: toll motorways (*autoroutes à péage*) 130km/h; dual carriageways/ divided roads and toll-free *auto-routes* 110km/h; other roads 90km/h; built-up areas 50km/h.

Unleaded petrol (*sans plomb*) is widely available. On-the-spot drink-driving fines are rightly severe. Under-10s should travel in the rear seats, and the wearing of all seat belts fitted in the car is compulsory.

If you plan to rent a car, it is cheaper to arrange it before departure. The major companies are represented in Provence.

You will need a current full (not provisional or learner's) driver's licence and, if you are bringing your own car, the original copy of the registration document and a current insurance certificate. You are required by law to have a hazard warning triangle if you have no hazard lights, a spare set of headlight bulbs and a national identity sticker. You may also want to fit beam deflectors to your headlights.

## *Electricity*

220 volts, with the Continental two-pin round plugs.

## *Embassies and Consulates*

**Australia:** 4 rue Jean-Rey, 75724 Paris, Cedex 15 (tel: (1) 40 59 33 00).
**Canada:** 35 avenue Montaigne, 75008 Paris (tel: (01) 47 23 01 01).
**Ireland:** 12 avenue Foch, 75116 Paris (tel: (1) 45 00 20 87).
**New Zealand:** 7 rue Léonard-da-Vinci, 75016 Paris (tel: (1) 45 00 24 11).
**UK:** 35 rue du Faubourg St-Honoré, 75383 Paris, Cedex 08, and its consular section at 9 avenue Hoche, 75008 Paris (tel: (1) 42 66 38 10); 24 avenue du Prado, 13006 Marseille (tel: 91 53 43 32).
**US:** 2 avenue Gabriel, 75382 Paris, Cedex 08 (tel: (1) 42 96 12 02/42 61 80 75); 12 boulevard Paul-Peytral, 13286 Marseille (tel: 91 54 92 00).

## *Health*

No vaccinations are required. EC citizens should obtain form E111 (from post offices) before departure to be eligible for free treatment or reduced medical costs. It is quite safe to drink the tap water served in hotels and restaurants; but never drink from a tap labelled *eau non potable*.

## *Holidays*

National public holidays, when banks and stores may close and trains run on the *jours fériés* timetable, are:
1 January, New Year's Day; Easter Monday; Ascension Day; Whit Monday; 1 May, Labour Day; 8 May, VE Day; 14 July, Bastille Day; 15 August, Assumption; 1 November, All Saints' Day; 11 November, Armistice Day; 25 December, Christmas Day.

## *Hotels and Restaurants*

Despite the inflated prices which are often synonymous with the South of France, it is possible to eat and sleep in Provence and still keep within most budgets – from Riviera five-star luxury to rural *auberges de jeunesse* (youth hostels).

### Sleeping

Independent travel has many advantages, particularly off-season,

**Provence scenery on the road to Nîmes**

but arriving at a tourist office and expecting to book a room for the night can be a gamble in most of high-season Provence, and out of the question on the Riviera.

Tourist offices (*syndicats d'initiative*) will give out lists of hotels in nearby towns, so a *télécarte* is a good investment. To book before going to France, contact your local French Government Tourist Office or the departmental tourist boards in Provence (see page 117). In addition, many of the French and international hotel chains accept reservations through central offices.

Hotel classifications are made by the government, and prices should be displayed in the lobby as well as on the back of the bedroom door. Most prices do not include breakfast, which you may or may not choose to take in the hotel.

### Eating

Provence has some of France's most renowned restaurants, in places where you would expect to find them – the promenade des Anglais in Nice and the rue de la République in Avignon – as well as in tiny inland villages. Location and high prices are no guarantee of good food, however, and you will pay for a sea view. Inland towns often have many restaurants in the old quarter, with a choice of several places: take time to

116

study menus first. Local recommendations are always useful.

Provence is an ideal region to discover local specialities, from a Marseille *bouillabaisse* to a dripping *pan bagnat*. Younger travellers who might not appreciate *aïoli* and *tapenade* will be relieved to see fast-food restaurants in larger towns and – a more local speciality – pizza, available nearly everywhere. If you are keeping to a budget, choose from the *prix fixe* menus, as these are generally very good value.

## Lost Property

Report loss of valuables to the police and obtain a copy of the statement for making an insurance claim. Cancel lost credit cards and travellers' cheques immediately. A lost passport should be reported at once to your nearest embassy or consulate, which will also issue emergency documents.

## Media and Entertainment

For a taste of local political, social and sporting issues as well as up-to-date entertainment information, daily newspapers such as *La Marseillaise*, *Le Provençal*, *Nice-Matin* and *Var-Matin* provide another perspective on Provençal life. The weekly *Semaine des Spectacles* lists plays and films for the region; if you want to watch an English-language film with

**Grape-picking in the Côte du Rhône wine region**

subtitles rather than dubbing, look out for *version originale*, or *vo*.

## Money Matters

The French franc (F or ff) is divided into 100 centimes. Notes are in denominations of 20F, 50F, 100F and 500F, and coins of 5, 10, 20 and 50 centimes, 1F, 2F, 5F, 10F and 20F.

It is best not to rely on one form of money alone. Not every hotelier will accept Eurocheques (for which you pay an annual fee to your bank), although you can use your card for cash withdrawals at Crédit Mutuel banks; Visa credit cards should be accepted everywhere there is a Carte Bleue sign; carrying travellers' cheques means your money is insured. Keep your money, cheques and credit cards separate, and make sure you keep a note of cheque and card numbers as well as telephone numbers to call if they are lost or stolen.

## Opening Times

Smaller stores, and even supermarkets in some towns, keep to traditional hours, closing for a two-hour lunch break and all day Mondays, although they may stay open until 7 or 8pm. Street markets also tend to finish by lunchtime, which will often mean buying food for a picnic lunch well before you plan to eat. Department stores and shops in large cities often stay open all day. Bank hours also vary, with some closing on Mondays and opening on Saturdays, while rural branches may open only once or twice a week. Be prepared for national holidays, when banks can close for up to three days. Most museums and monuments in Provence also close on either Monday or Tuesday.

## Pharmacies

Recognisable by the sign of the green cross, pharmacies offer reliable medical advice, and the rota of late-night duty chemists is printed in local newspapers. In Nice, an all-night service is given at the Pharmacie Principale at 10 rue Masséna (tel: 93 87 85 48). Many stock familiar brands of disposable nappies (*couches*), tampons and sanitary towels (*serviettes hygiéniques*), which can also be bought from supermarkets, and increasingly nowadays there are dispensing machines for condoms (*préservatifs*) installed outside pharmacies.

## Places of Worship

Catholic churches are found in every town and village. Ask tourist offices about other local churches. There are synagogues in Avignon, Carpentras and Cavaillon.

## Police and Emergencies

In cities and towns, police duties are carried out by the *Police Municipale* (wearing blue uniforms). The countryside and smaller places are covered by the national police force of *Gendarmes* (blue trousers, black jackets and white belts). Both should be addressed with courtesy should you want their help and particularly if they should want yours. On-the-spot fines for traffic offences are the norm and can be hefty.

To call an ambulance or the police in an emergency, dial **17**; for the fire services, dial **18**.

## Post Offices

Generally known as *La Poste* or the PTT, and recognisable by their yellow signs, post offices can get extremely busy and should be avoided if all you want are stamps (*timbres-postes*), which you can buy from *tabacs*. However, they are useful for services such as photocopying and are invaluable for exchanging money on days such as public holidays when the banks are closed.

## Public Transport

In general, public transport is an excellent way to discover France. Train and bus services are frequent along the Côte d'Azur, and though it takes determination to explore the more remote parts of inland Provence without a car, it can be a rewarding way to travel, particularly as you will meet more people *en route*. Buses are operated by local private companies, with routes often reflecting market days and serving the smaller villages surrounding towns. Longer distances are generally covered more quickly and cheaply by train, with services operated by SNCF (*Société Nationale des Chemins de Fer*), the French state railway. For details before you leave, contact SNCF at 179 Piccadilly, London W1V 0BA, tel: (071) 491–1573 or 226/230 Westchester Avenue, White Plains, New York 10604 (tel: (914) 681–322) and in Provence at avenue Thiers, Nice (tel: 93 87 50 50).

## Senior Citizens

Independent travellers who wish to qualify for reduced fares on public transport and entrance fees can buy a *Carte Vermeille* for around 80 to 90F from SNCF stations. Even without the card, most museums offer a *tarif réduit* (reduced tariff) for senior citizens.

## Student and Youth Travel

British travellers of any age can buy an InterRail card, although the under-26 ticket remains the cheapest, offering 4 weeks' train travel throughout Europe for £180; the American Eurail card offers a similar deal. InterRail is also valid for free travel on those SNCF bus routes that have replaced a previous rail route.

International Student Identity Cards (ISIC) are invaluable in qualifying for reduced entrance fees to museums and monuments, while for cheap accommodation, the *Foyers des Jeunes Travailleurs* are useful alternatives to youth hostels *(auberges de jeunesse)*. Write in advance for addresses (in summer reservations are essential) to the *Chambre Départmentale de Tourisme*.

## Telephones

A few public telephones *(cabines)* remain coin-operated, and it is possible to make metered calls from booths in larger post offices, but the great majority of French public telephones now take *télécartes*, which you can buy in 50 or 120 units from *tabacs* and post offices. All French numbers have eight digits whether you are dialling locally or to another *département*, but if you are calling Paris from the provinces, add the prefix 16-1. You can call abroad from any *cabine* with the sign of a blue bell; for Britain dial 19 (tone changes) 44, then the number minus the initial 0; for the US and Canada the code is 19-1.

Instructions for using the card phones are generally written in English as well as French. If not, insert the card and close the shutter when you are instructed *fermez le volet*.

Cheaper rates apply after 8pm and all day at weekends. Calling from your hotel room is the most expensive option of all.

## Time

France observes Central European Time, which is one hour ahead of Greenwich Mean Time from late

September to late March, and two hours ahead for the rest of the year.

## Tipping

Your restaurant meals and hotel room will almost certainly be *service compris* (service included), and tipping is at your discretion, but taxi drivers, porters, hairdressers and others providing a service should be tipped as you would at home. Also watch out for the attendants with saucers in public toilets, where the amount expected is usually displayed.

## Toilets

Tiny hilltop villages may have a pristine public toilet in the square next to the church, while in large cities you could walk blocks to find a concrete *toilette*, whose sliding metal doors and musical accompaniment have replaced the cast-iron *pissoirs* in French townscapes. There is no general rule, except perhaps to use one when you see one. Museums and fast-food restaurants are reliable alternatives to the old standby, the pavement café; buying a drink might seem to defeat the object, but is often expected, and you may have to ask for the key *(la clé)* at the bar. Don't be surprised if you encounter a hole with foot plates (watch out for the flush button). The toilets on the harbour at St-Tropez are some of the most unpleasant, and expensive, in the South of France.

**One of Provence's pleasures: watching the world go by**

## Tourist Offices

Whether you want a street plan, festival details or lists of hotels and restaurants, the French Government *Offices de Tourisme*, also known as *Syndicats d'Initiative* (SI), are an invaluable source of current local information and a good place to start your visit in most French towns and cities. To plan your trip in advance, contact the French Government Tourist Office (FGTO) at:
178 Piccadilly, London W1V 0AL (tel: (071) 491-7622);
610 Fifth Avenue, New York, NY 10020 (tel: (212) 757-1125);
Suite 490, 1981 Avenue McGill College, Montréal, Québec H3A 2W9 (tel: (514) 873-2015).

But local tourist offices are often far more helpful, and you may prefer to write direct to the *Chambre Départementale de Tourisme* (CDT) offices:
**Vaucluse:** La Balance, place Campana, BP 147, 84008 Avignon Cedex (tel: 90 86 43 42);
**Bouches-du-Rhône:** 6 rue du Jeune-Anacharsis, 13001 Marseille, (tel: 91 54 92 66);
**Var:** 1 boulevard Clemenceau, 83303 Draguignan (tel: 94 68 63 30);
**Alpes-de-Haute Provence:** Rond Point et Tampinet, 04000 Digne (tel: 92 31 42 73);
**Alpes-Maritimes:** 55 Promenade des Anglais, 06000 Nice (tel: 93 44 50 59).

# •GLOSSARY•

English is spoken by those involved in tourist trades and in the larger cosmopolitan towns – less so in smaller, rural places. Your efforts to speak French will always be appreciated. The most useful phrase in the French language is *s'il vous plaît* (please).

**Basic vocabulary**
yes oui
no non
hello/good morning bonjour
good evening bonsoir
goodbye au revoir
thank you (very much) merci (beaucoup/bien)
sorry pardon/excusez-moi
toilets les toilettes
no smoking défense de fumer
entrance entrée
exit sortie
later plus tard
now maintenant
today aujourd'hui
yesterday hier
tomorrow demain
week une semaine
when? quand?
why? pourquoi?
with avec
without sans
prohibited interdit
closed fermé
open ouvert
big grand
small petit
bad mauvais
cold froid
hot chaud

**Types of shops**
bakery la boulangerie
butcher la boucherie
cake shop la pâtisserie
chemist la pharmacie
cheese shop la fromagerie
delicatessen la charcuterie
fishmonger la poissonnerie
food shop l'alimentation
grocers' l'épicerie
hairdresser le coiffeur
library la bibliothèque
market le marché
newsagent/stationer la librairie
post office le bureau de poste
supermarket le supermarché
sweet shop la confiserie

**Eating and drinking**
beer/draught une bière/pression
coffee un café
black/white noir/au lait
decaffeinated décaféiné
hot chocolate chocolat chaud
milk lait
mineral water l'eau minérale

tea/lemon tea un thé/au citron
herb tea infusion/tisane
wine – white/red le vin – blanc/ rouge
wine list la carte des vins

fixed price menu prix fixe
all included service compris
a little more encore un peu
butter le beurre
can I have the bill? l'addition, s'il vous plaît?
cheese fromage
closed...Monday fermeture...lundi
dessert les desserts
first course hors d'ouevre
have you got a table? avez-vous une table de libre?
I would like/we would like je voudrais/on voudrait
second course entrée
medium rare à point
menu la carte
rare saignant
salt sel
self service libre service (le self)
snacks casse-croûte
all day à toute heure
to eat manger
to drink boire
very rare bleu
well done bien cuit
what do you recommend? qu'est-ce que vous recommandez?
where are the toilets? où sont les toilettes?

**Directions**
after après
behind derrière
before avant
here ici
in front of devant
left à gauche
near près
opposite en face de
right à droite
straight on tout droit
there là
where? où?
where is? où est?
where is the station? où est la gare?

**Travelling around**
bridge pont
bus autobus
bus stop arrêt
car park un parking
I am going to... je vais à...
I need... j'ai besoin de...
I want to get off je voudrais descendre
my car has broken down ma voiture est en panne
oil huile
parking prohibited
petrol essence

petrol station poste d'essence
platform quai
plane avion
please direct me to... pour aller à...s'il vous plaît
railway station la gare
the road for la route pour
ticket office vente de billets
to cross the road traverser la rue
traffic lights les feux
tyres les pneus
underground Métro

**Phrases**
at what time? à quelle heure?
call an ambulance appelez une ambulance, s'il vous plaît
could you speak more slowly pouvez-vous parler plus lentement, s'il vous plaît
do you speak English? parlez-vous anglais?
help! au secours!
how much is this? combien?
I do not understand je ne comprends pas
I need a doctor je voudrais voir un docteur
I want... je voudrais...
please could you write it down? pouvez-vous me l'écrire?
where is the nearest police station? où est le post de police le plus proche?

**Numbers**
one un
two deux
three trois
four quatre
five cinq
six six
seven sept
eight huit
nine neuf
ten dix
first premier (-ière)
second seconde (deuxième)
third troisième
fourth quatrième
fifth cinquième

**Days of the week**
Monday lundi
Tuesday mardi
Wednesday mercredi
Thursday jeudi
Friday vendredi
Saturday samedi
Sunday dimanche

**Months of the year**
January janvier
February février
March mars
April avril
May mai
June juin
July juillet
August août
September septembre
October octobre
November novembre
December décembre

# ·INDEX·

# ACKNOWLEDGEMENTS

The Automobile Association wishes to thank the following photographers and libraries for their assistance in the preparation of this book.

RICK STRANGE was commissioned to take the photographs for this book and they appear on the following pages.
1, 3, 4/5, 6a, 12, 13a, 13b, 14, 16, 19, 20, 22, 23a, 23b, 24a, 25, 26, 27, 28a, 28/9, 30, 31, 33, 34, 35a, 35b, 36, 37a, 37b, 38a, 38b, 39, 40a, 40b, 41, 42a, 42b, 43, 44a, 45, 46, 47, 48a, 48b, 49, 50a, 50b, 51a, 51b, 54, 55, 56, 57, 58b, 60, 62, 63a, 63b, 64, 65, 66, 68, 69, 71, 73, 74a, 74b, 75, 78, 80a, 81, 84b, 85, 86b, 87, 89, 91, 92, 93a, 93b, 95, 97, 98, 99, 100, 102b, 104, 105, 107, 108/9, 109a, 110, 114, 115, 116, 117

The remaining photographs are from the following libraries.

AA PHOTO LIBRARY
Tony Oliver 79b, 84a, 94
Neil Ray 10a, 10b
Barrie Smith 8b, 18, 24b, 32, 52a, 52b, 53, 58a, 67, 70, 80b, 82a, 88

J ALLAN CASH PHOTOLIBRARY 8a St Raphaël, 77 red rocks near St Raphaël, 82b cathedral in Toulon, 83 Toulon Quay, 96 Golfe-Juan, 106a Isola 2000, 106b Isola 2000 skiing

MARY EVANS PICTURE LIBRARY 6b Charlemagne, 7 Napoleon I

RICHARD SALE 86a Nice, 102a Nice

SPECTRUM COLOUR LIBRARY 11 Marseille old harbour, 76a Roquebrune-sur-Argens, 76b St Raphaël, 79a Ste-Maxime, 90 Beaulieu-sur-Mer harbour

WORLD PICTURES Cover Provence scenery

ZEFA PICTURE LIBRARY 44b Peaches and Pears painting